THE GENERATION
THAT SEEKS THE LORD

THE GENERATION
THAT SEEKS THE LORD

GARY WILKERSON

An Expository Devotional on the Psalms

VOLUME 2
Psalms 13-21

Ambassador International
Greenville, South Carolina & Belfast, Northern Ireland
www.ambassador-international.com

The Generation That Seeks the Lord
An Expository Devotional on the Psalms, Volume 2

Gary Wilkerson
©2025 by World Challenge, Inc.
All rights reserved

ISBN: 978-1-64960-731-7, hardcover
ISBN: 978-1-64960-880-2, paperback
eISBN: 978-1-64960-769-0

Cover design by Efrain Garcia
Interior Typesetting by Dentelle Design
Edited by Katie Cruice Smith and Lindsey Jones

No part of this publication may be reproduced, distributed, or transmitted in any form or by any means, including photocopying, recording, or other electronic or mechanical methods, without the prior written permission of the publisher, except in the case of brief quotations embodied in critical reviews and certain other noncommercial uses permitted by copyright law. For permission requests, contact the publisher using the information below.

Unless otherwise indicated, all Scripture quotations are from the English Standard Version.® Copyright © 2001 by Crossway Bibles, a publishing ministry of Good News Publishers. Used by permission. All rights reserved.

Scripture quotations marked NIV are from the Holy Bible, New International Version®, NIV® Copyright ©1973, 1978, 1984, 2011 by Biblica, Inc.® Used by permission. All rights reserved worldwide.

Ambassador International titles may be purchased in bulk for education, business, fundraising, or sales promotional use. For information, please email sales@emeraldhouse.com.

AMBASSADOR INTERNATIONAL	AMBASSADOR BOOKS
Emerald House	The Mount
411 University Ridge, Suite B14	2 Woodstock Link
Greenville, SC 29601	Belfast, BT6 8DD
United States	Northern Ireland, United Kingdom
www.ambassador-international.com	www.ambassadormedia.co.uk

The colophon is a trademark of Ambassador, a Christian publishing company.

Table of Contents

INTRODUCTION 1

CHAPTER ONE
PSALM 13
WILL YOU FORGET ME FOREVER? 3

CHAPTER TWO
PSALM 14
THE GENERATION OF THE RIGHTEOUS 17

CHAPTER THREE
PSALM 15
WHO CAN STAND BEFORE A HOLY GOD? 31

CHAPTER FOUR
PSALM 16
THE PRESERVATION OF THE SAINTS 43

CHAPTER FIVE
PSALM 17A
A CRY FOR JUSTICE 63

CHAPTER SIX
PSALM 17B
A HEART AFTER GOD 77

CHAPTER SEVEN
PSALM 18A
VICTORY OVER DEATH, THE DEVIL, AND THE GRAVE 91

CHAPTER EIGHT
PSALM 18B
THE LORD IS MY ROCK
AND MY FORTRESS 111

CHAPTER NINE
PSALM 18C
MO(U)RNING HAS BROKEN 125

CHAPTER TEN
PSALM 19
THE LAW OF THE LORD IS PERFECT 145

CHAPTER ELEVEN
PSALM 20
CHANGING LIVES THROUGH PRAYER 157

CHAPTER TWELVE
PSALM 21
THE FAVOR AND THE FIRE OF JESUS 171

BIOGRAPHY 185
BIBLIOGRAPHY 187

Introduction

JESUS IS ALL OVER THE Psalms. If Psalms were just a book of poems about grief, encouragement, the Lord's protection, and overcoming enemies, it would still be a valuable asset to every believer. However, these 150 chapters are dense with content about Jesus. Although He is not named, He is present in every chapter. He is in the shepherd's heart; He is the strong tower; He is the Deliverer; He is the Comforter of those downtrodden.

At times, I see so much of Jesus in the Psalms that I wonder if we could include it in the New Testament. I have tried to write this book to highlight the hero of Psalms, and the hero is more than David. It is Israel; and more than that, it is Jesus.

This second volume covers Psalms 13-21. Hopefully, God will grant me the grace and the time to complete each of the twelve-chapter volumes. I consider this book to be an expository devotional. Expository teaching is an in-depth study of the text, while devotional writing moves the heart by applying the insights gained from the exposited, scriptural text.

I pray that your mind will be instructed and your heart set ablaze as a result of reading this book. I also pray that you will take the time not just to read the chapters but also to pause after each chapter and meditate, pray, and journal about what God is revealing to you.

EVERY BLESSING,
Gary Wilkerson

CHAPTER ONE

Psalm 13
Will You Forget Me Forever?

1 How long, O Lord? Will you forget me forever?
   How long will you hide your face from me?
2 How long must I take counsel in my soul
   and have sorrow in my heart all the day?
   How long shall my enemy be exalted over me?
3 Consider and answer me, O Lord my God;
   light up my eyes, lest I sleep the sleep of death,
4 lest my enemy say, "I have prevailed over him,"
   lest my foes rejoice because I am shaken.
5 But I have trusted in your steadfast love;
   my heart shall rejoice in your salvation.
6 I will sing to the Lord,
   because he has dealt bountifully with me.

IN THE FIRST THREE VERSES of this Psalm, David asked, "How long?" four times. In Scripture, when we see a phrase repeated, it signals to us that something significant is being said. Four times, David uttered an anguished cry from his broken heart: "How long, O Lord?" He was saying, in essence, "My wounded soul is downcast to the depths. How long will you leave me in this state, O God?" The question "How long, O Lord?"

is asked over sixty times throughout Scripture, appearing in several books of the Bible. Obviously, it speaks of the anguish of struggling saints. Surely, you've had seasons when you cried out, "Lord, how long will I have this pain in my body?" "How long will this relationship be broken?" "How long will I be in dire financial straits?" "How long will this depression afflict my mind?" "How long until your promises for my life become a reality?" These questions reflect realities for virtually everyone who follows Jesus.

"WILL YOU FORGET ME FOREVER?" (PSALM 13:1)

The Hebrew word for "forever" in this verse suggests two dimensions. One is the eternality, or permanence, of forever. The other is the utterness, or finality, of forever. One dimension speaks of a length of time, and the other speaks of depths. David was anguished by his sense of both when he cried, "Lord, I know you have forgotten me. So, is it all over for me now?"

It's one thing to be forgotten for an hour or a day, as when a friend promises to pick you up to go somewhere. If they don't show up for a long while, at least you have an end in mind as to when they'll finally remember you. It's a whole other matter, however, when days, weeks, or months pass by and you wonder whether your friend has abandoned you for good.

This was how Joseph must have felt when he was imprisoned by Potiphar after being falsely accused. If he had been jailed for a few days or weeks, maybe he wouldn't have felt forgotten or abandoned; but month after month passed. Spending season after season in prison made him begin to despair. As his cellmates were released, Joseph pleaded with them to tell Pharaoh about him so he could be released, too, but the cellmates forgot about him after they got out. "The chief cupbearer did not remember Joseph, but forgot him" (Gen. 40:23).

So it can be with us at times. We pray to God with all our heart, yet we feel forgotten. We receive counsel from friends; but afterward, we feel forgotten by them. We spend sleepless nights over these things, feeling utterly forgotten. Day after day, we feel the eternality of being forgotten, the length and forever-ness of it, and it brings us distress. After a while, the *depths* of being forgotten begins to sink in; and we may start to despair. Sometimes, I wonder if David's questions may be the saddest in all of Scripture. "Will you forget me eternally and utterly? Am I permanently lost to you?"

A SENSE OF FORGOTTENNESS

How many times has a child felt forgotten when their distracted parent forgot to pick them up from school? How many kids have been forgotten by a separated parent who was supposed to host them up for the weekend but never showed up? How many children's spirits wither as they sit on the stoop of their home watching neighborhood kids pass by without so much as a "hi"? How often has the child of an alcoholic parent been overlooked, neglected, despised, or abused? How many adults have spent hours in church, at a party, or at any kind of gathering and never been greeted with a single "hello" or welcomed with an extended hand?

There are deeper, more frightening worries lying beneath the question, "How long will I be forgotten?" Underlying this are worries, such as, "Will anybody ever care for me?" "Am I all alone in this world?" "Why is no one ever there for me?" "Have I been abandoned completely?" "Why isn't there anyone for me to delight in and for them to delight in me?"

Our ministry once received a letter that stated simply, "I need a hug." At first glance, this kind of request may seem trite. As the letter went on, however, the power of the writer's need became clear. They continued, "Not just any hug. I want a long-lasting hug. I want someone to get hold of me and hug me tight, so tight that I forget the sad things in my life. I want to cry on the shoulder of someone without being asked any questions. I want to hug them back so hard that they understand my pain. I need someone to tell me that I'll be okay. I need a hug that makes me forget everything I have to think about all day long, every day. I desperately need that hug."

Another letter described an experience that stunned me. The person wrote, "I feel so lonely all of the time. I try to reach out to people and be social, but no one ever reciprocates. Even my parents sometimes don't return my calls. They can't seem to be bothered. I called to see if they wanted to get together for dinner sometime convenient for them in the coming weeks or even months. They answered, 'We'll have to check our schedule.' I never heard back from them."

A LONGING TO BE LOVED

Feeling forgotten doesn't mean you've done something wrong. It reveals a passionate heart to love and be loved. That desire is not wrong or selfish. It reveals your God-given desire to connect, to be part of a community, and to stay in relationships. The cry of "How long, O Lord?" isn't the cry of someone who lacks faith; it's the heart-desire of someone with a strong passion for relationship. It's normal to look in the mirror and say, "I feel lonely right now." You wouldn't feel lonely if you didn't care.

Some people try to deny or bury the lonely feelings that arise in them. They react by deciding, "I'll just binge on another TV show," or "I don't need anyone around in order to enjoy a good book." Over time, that kind of avoidance can lead to a calloused heart. When we're lonely and have no one to reach out to, we may turn to the Holy Spirit to seek comfort and to reflect honestly. We can pray, "Lord, don't let my heart go dormant about my lack of relationships. Awaken in me a genuine desire to connect with people and to find a good friend." More often than not, it is our continued longings that lead us to the relationships we desire.

David had the same sorrowful longings we have, except that he had them about God. He raised a deep question when he asked, "How long will you hide your face from me?" (Psalm 13:1). We may be randomly forgotten by someone, but it's worse when they actually hide their face from us. Have you ever walked down a corridor at work only to have a coworker look away before making eye contact? What takes place inside you when that happens? All kinds of inner alarms go off about your self-worth. You can't help feeling like there's something wrong, that you've done something to offend them or that they just don't like your company.

For David, the problem wasn't that a person was hiding their face from him; it was God Himself doing so. Have you ever felt that the Lord not only forgot and abandoned you but that He purposely hid His face from you? This could never be true of God because He never stops loving you. Even before you knew Him—while you were still in sin, opposing God or seeing Him as your Enemy—He loved you and gave His life for you. "But God shows his love for us in that while we were still sinners, Christ died for us" (Rom. 5:8).

God is near you; sometimes, you just don't feel it. That doesn't mean He has turned His face from you. The great preacher C.H. Spurgeon said, "A hidden face is not a sign of a forgetful heart." The Lord certainly doesn't hide His faithful heart from us, nor does He have a forgetful heart. If we feel He has forgotten us, we can be sure He's doing a kingdom work in us because His love for us never stops; it has always been there. His current work in you may be a kind of purification meant to create in you a hunger you don't have. In other words, He may be reestablishing your passions and desires or shaping in you a core conviction that you need to fulfill your high calling.

Often when we feel abandoned, we think our only option is to turn to our own counsel. Turning to our own counsel may seem reasonable to us. In fact, it can look like our only option; but in truth, it can be dangerous. David fell into this trap. He thought he had to figure out his problems for himself. Later on in the Psalms, he wrote of discovering a better path. "I bless the Lord who gives me counsel; in the night also my heart instructs me" (Psalm 16:7). In that Psalm, David knew that morning would come, suggesting an awakening to God's continual presence.

Even though the Lord is with us all the time, we can feel a lack of His presence; and that's when we're tempted to turn to our own resources. We tell ourselves, "I'll figure out my marriage problems." "I'll figure out a way to get a promotion." "I'll figure out my future." The reformer John Calvin said such self-counsel wasn't really counsel of any kind but was actually worry. He literally translated "counsel" as "worry" in David's verse, "How long must I take counsel in my soul" (Psalm 13:2). Calvin said the result of such self-counsel is that people torment themselves with endless thoughts. The greater danger, he noted, was that people's anxieties and fears compelled them to change their purposes in life. When they lost a sense of control, they took measures to regain it; and that was disastrous. C.H. Spurgeon echoed this, saying, "Our ways of escape become innumerable, but none prevail."[1]

We can't possibly work out the kingdom path that God alone can orchestrate. I think of our self-driven strategies as the spawning of a multitude of carnal ideas. We want to merely solve our dilemmas, whereas God wants to transform them and to transform us through them, making all things new.

The way Psalm 13 was constructed tells us that David felt forgotten by God and thus turned to his own counsel. In our own lives, the reverse can be true. Sometimes we turn to our own counsel first; and because our actions are missing God's wisdom, we can end up feeling empty and forgotten by Him. In this case, we're the ones who do the forgetting. Maybe, then, God says of us, "How long will I be forgotten by you? How many days will go by before you enter my presence? How long will you think of your own counsel as sufficient instead of trusting me?" As one proverb famously advises, "In all your ways acknowledge him, and he will make straight your paths" (Prov. 3:6).

David then spoke of a sorrow that can follow when we rely on our own counsel. "How long must I take counsel in my soul and have sorrow in my heart all the day?" (Psalm 13:2). Turning to our own counsel does not result in peace and joy. That's because our own plotting denies God's wisdom; and without it, our hearts are going to sorrow. His heart

---

[1] Charles Haddon Spurgeon, *Spurgeon's Commentary: Hebrews* (Bellingham: Lexham Press, 2015).

contains the powerful solutions we seek, solutions He has already planned and formed.

SOMETHING PERSONAL AND RELATIONAL OR EVEN NATIONAL

David ended this verse by asking, "How long shall my enemy be exalted over me?" (Psalm 13:2). In David's case, his personal crises were also national crises. The enemies who came against him involved his own family, but the implications reached far into the political realm of the nation.

The opposing forces that each of us face today may be relational, or they may be more broadly national. In the US, I see a spiritual decline unlike any I've witnessed in my entire lifetime. In volume one of this series on the Psalms, we read about people who exalt wickedness as good. "On every side the wicked prowl, as vileness is exalted among the children of man" (Psalm 12:8). These forces protest against things that are good and promote legislation that lifts up evil.

Closer to home, your opponents may be a spouse who abuses you, a boss who overlooks you, a friend who betrays you, or a church that rejects you. In David's case, it is possible that his greatest enemy was his own despairing soul. Because his problems were so overwhelming and he sensed that God had abandoned him, David was nagged by the impulse to take control of his situation. He turned to his own strength to resolve his problems, and his thoughts are clear in Psalm 13: "God has turned his face from me, so now I guess it's all up to me."

When you're so down that you feel forgotten by God, your despairing soul can become a haunting enemy. You wound yourself with thoughts that swirl endlessly in search of a solution to your problems. Certain self-accusing thoughts repeat themselves with no resolution. It becomes a cruel, vicious, and never-ending cycle.

David continued, "Lest my enemy say, 'I have prevailed over him,' lest my foes rejoice because I am shaken" (Psalm 13:4). He was saying, in essence, "I'm so shaken by these things I face that I'm close to giving up. Enduring all of this is too hard because I feel like I'm left to do it all alone, by myself."

A KEY CHANGE FOR DAVID

"But I have trusted in your steadfast love; my heart shall rejoice in your salvation" (Psalm 13:5). This verse signaled that David had landed on a powerful revelation. In fact, a transformation took place. He went from feeling like God had turned His face away from him to rejoicing in the salvation that comes from the Lord. In fact, this verse foreshadows the power of Christ's cross to deliver us from any condition and to save us utterly.

How did this key change happen for David? As the verse states, he was saved from his own counsel by trusting in God's steadfast love. Though he didn't sense God's presence or direction, he knew God's love was immovable. That turned his heart around.

"I will sing to the Lord, because he has dealt bountifully with me" (Psalm 13:6). At this point, David trusted God again. He had gone from feeling forgotten by the Lord to feeling deeply loved by Him. He now felt the opposite of ignored and diminished; he felt the bounty of God's love. This was a major shift. David was no longer stuck; he was free, despite his pressing circumstances.

We see a specific shift in David in verse three. "Consider and answer me, O Lord my God; light up my eyes, lest I sleep the sleep of death" (Psalm 13:3). David was confessing, "Lord, if it were left to me, I would die. That's where I'm headed without you, because my own counsel leads me to a dark place. I ask you, Lord, please, light up my eyes. Let me see your salvation, and I'll have joy again. Let me know what a new song will sound like. Let me picture what faith and confidence will look like now. If you light up my eyes, this darkness will lift from me. I know that even in my most horrible circumstances, the light of your face shines on me. Lord, let me see!"

David was no longer just crying out his anguish. He was praying, seeking God for something. Instead of wallowing in a despair that feeds on itself, he called on the name of the Lord. He knew his only hope and solution lay in God.

TOO SIMPLISTIC OR EASY

You may ask, "Is that all? I'm just supposed to call on the Lord's name?" That is absolutely what you're to do. It is not complex. You don't need a master of divinity degree. God loves the simple cry of a broken heart, and He bends Himself to show His care. He picks you up and refreshes you, lightening your eyes in your darkened hour and beginning a new work in your life.

The kind of sorrow that David described can only be handled on our knees. This isn't just *a* solution; it is the only solution. Our cleverness will never get us out of our mess. David's key change came when he said, "Consider and answer me" (Psalm 13:3). The word "consider" means, "Look in my direction, Lord. Let your countenance shine on me." Imagine the brilliance of the light that appeared on the Mount of Transfiguration, when the disciples saw Jesus talking with Moses and Elijah. That kind of light transforms everything by showing us the ultimate reality behind everything.

The word "consider" can also mean to respond, scrutinize, or speak a word. The prophet Isaiah called on God for this. "Look down from heaven and see, from your holy and beautiful habitation. Where are your zeal and your might? The stirring of your inner parts and your compassion are held back from me" (Isa. 63:15). The prophet was asking the Lord, "Look down on me and bring these things." His first request of God was to bring might, but he also asked the Lord to bring compassion. Both of these things—strength and omnipotence and mercy and kindness—are married in Christ.

Like Isaiah, when we call on the name of the Lord, we ask Him to bring newness of life. We want Him to scrutinize our situation and bring His solution so that we don't stay stuck in our anxieties. His solution for us holds transforming power.

CLOSE PARALLELS TO PAUL'S LETTER TO THE EPHESIANS

Note how close Paul's phrasing is to David's in Ephesians 1:18: "Having the eyes of your hearts enlightened, that you may know what is the hope to which he has called you, what are the riches of his glorious inheritance in the saints." There it is again: "Lord, lighten the eyes of our hearts." To what are our eyes enlightened? According to Paul, they are opened to hope. God's light gives us eternal hope in our most hopeless situation. This is our key change so that we can say as David did, "I have new hope that God is hearing me, answering me, and drawing near to me." With this verse, Paul wanted us to know the power of Heaven that stands behind our hope: "What is the immeasurable greatness of his power toward us who believe, according to the working of his great might" (Ephesians 1:19).

The Greek word that Paul uses for "eyes" in Ephesians 1:18 is *pho*. This is the root of the word "photograph." Photos show us a new way to see; they lay out a vision before us that we may not have pictured before. In addition, the word "enlightened" is presented in the perfect tense. In grammatical terms, this signifies an action that has been completed, finished, and perfected. It means that the enlightening of the eyes of our heart has already been done for us. So if you have received Jesus as your Savior and Lord, you have been enlightened. This enlightening not only has been accomplished for you but also continues to exist in the present moment.

Being enlightened also means that it has happened *to* us, that we aren't the agents to make it happen. The world would have us believe otherwise, claiming that we alone can generate for ourselves a better outlook on life. We're urged to improve our perspective on things, to see the glass as half-full instead of half-empty. Both Isaiah and Paul testify, however, that this is the work of the Holy Spirit; He does this for us, and the work is continual.

THE TRANSFORMATIVE KEY THAT WILL CHANGE YOUR LIFE

The act of calling on the Lord shifts us out of darkness and into light. He enables us to see a brighter future in the midst of a darker day. This change is not only mental but also emotional, spiritual, and even physical. It begins as an internal change; and as our heart is transformed, so are our environment and circumstances as we walk in confident faith that we are loved.

Is your heart stuck in despair? Are you unable to see anything beyond circumstances that cause you to despair? Let the grace of God enlighten your eyes to bring greater light not only to you but also to the world in which you move. Through your transformation, the Spirit brings change to others—from friends and family to culture and society. He also brings His glorious salvation by quickening your faith and convicting others of His piercing love.

You don't have to worry or fear over your circumstances. You don't have to listen to the voice of despair. You can begin to sing a new song. You can have joy and laughter again because the Lord deals bountifully with you. Just call on His name.

CHAPTER TWO

Psalm 14

The Generation of the Righteous

1 The fool says in his heart, "There is no God."
   They are corrupt, they do abominable deeds;
   there is none who does good.
2 The Lord looks down from heaven on the children of man,
   to see if there are any who understand,
   who seek after God.
3 They have all turned aside; together they have become corrupt;
   there is none who does good,
   not even one.
4 Have they no knowledge, all the evildoers
   who eat up my people as they eat bread
   and do not call upon the Lord?
5 There they are in great terror,
   for God is with the generation of the righteous.
6 You would shame the plans of the poor,
   but the Lord is his refuge.
7 Oh, that salvation for Israel would come out of Zion!
   When the Lord restores the fortunes of his people,
   let Jacob rejoice, let Israel be glad.

VERSE FIVE GIVES US THE title of this chapter. We live in the generation of the righteous, and having God with us is essential in an hour when "there is none who does good, not even one" (Psalm 14:3). This Psalm shows the great contrast between a people steeped in wickedness, corruption, and rebellion toward God and a people who are God-inspired, God-touched, God-fueled, and God-ordained to be worshipers and serve Him in righteousness. This latter group is a royal priesthood set apart for His purposes; and Psalm 14 shows us that such a generation always lives alongside a vile generation, with the two groups often clashing and contending with one another.

REALITIES RECOGNIZED BY THE GENERATION OF THE RIGHTEOUS

The first reality that the generation of the righteous understands is that they live amid a crooked generation. Second, they have seen many of the righteous fall away from faith. Third, they vigilantly watch over their own hearts to strengthen their faith against the constant tide of evil. Fourth, their existence strikes terror in the hearts of the wicked. Fifth and finally, they cry out for spiritual awakening, deliverance, freedom, and salvation for themselves, their neighbors, and their nation. As they consider these realities, their only desires are to be fruitful and to walk in all that God tells them to do. The result of their commitment is a life of amazing joy, gladness, and worship.

Let's start with the first reality. "The fool says in his heart, 'There is no God.' They are corrupt, they do abominable deeds; there is none who does good" (Psalm 14:1). In this verse, David pointed out a regression among the wicked. First, they don't believe in God. As a result, their hearts become corrupt. In turn, their actions become abominable.

The apostle Paul described this same decline in his letter to the Romans, as the surrounding culture moved from unbelief to depraved minds to abominable actions. Paul summed up this regression in one verse. "And since they did not see fit to acknowledge God, God gave them up to a debased mind to do what ought not to be done" (Rom. 1:28).

We see this very declension all around us today. As more and more populations of nations drift away from faith, their cultures change significantly. Their governments pass legislation to support ungodliness; their education systems incorporate vile teachings; and their entertainment becomes more brazenly dark. It's not hard to see this happening in America. There's a widespread move away from faith toward worldliness and ungodliness, and the result is a flood of filth spreading through the land.

The generation of the righteous is not surprised by this. In fact, they do not expect things to be otherwise. That is one of their sober realizations. They pray that God will move mightily, and they work for righteousness in their community and city; but they fully realize that they live in a fallen world. Therefore, they're not surprised when they see wickedness thriving around them. Nor do they cower in fear as they see evil prevailing. The rapid falling away of their brethren does not send them spiraling into despair. They don't worry that they're too small a minority to have any effect on the way things are. They're neither dismayed nor overwhelmed, and they don't think the situation is hopeless.

On the contrary, in such times, the generation of the righteous are as bold as lions. Nothing that happens around them diminishes their faith. I encourage you in turn not to be surprised when the world acts like the world. Sin follows sin, and it grows worse and more abominable in God's sight. This is a fact, and David states it as such. His psalms were written to be sung by the people of God, so Psalm 14 clearly served as both a warning and an encouragement to followers of the Lord.

PAUL'S QUOTE OF PSALM 14 TO REINFORCE HIS MESSAGE

"As it is written: 'None is righteous, no, not one; no one understands; no one seeks for God. All have turned aside; together they have become worthless; no one does good, not even one'" (Rom. 3:10-12). The underlying message here is that evil persists in generation after generation and will continue to do so until Jesus returns with judgment and righteousness. In the meantime, there will always be contention between the wicked and the righteous.

Another underlying message is that the generation before us included a holy remnant who stood strong in faith. Now it is our turn to stand strong. Personally, I'm not afraid of what my children and grandchildren may have to face. God knew what this hour would hold, and He is faithful to equip the younger generation just as He equips us. I would even say to you that our young ones were born for such a time as this, to be salt and light in an hour of darkness and perversion. I am hopeful for every young person of God who is determined to stand faithful no matter what happens in society.

By comparison, my generation, the baby boomers, grew up in a culture of materialism, and that spirit crept into the church in insidious ways. Christians, by the millions, adopted a "prosperity gospel" that aimed to teach us we could have whatever we desired. This was a teaching of comfort; and when comfort didn't come, those who embraced the deadly doctrine were alarmed. Some became disillusioned, falling away from faith altogether, tragically embittered over life's trials and hardships.

Psalm 14 calls us to be a different kind of people today. We are called to stand faithfully on the pure and powerful Word of God to see us through and to see His faithfulness awesomely displayed.

PAUL'S ADVICE TO TIMOTHY ABOUT CORRUPTION

> But understand this, that in the last days there will come times of difficulty. For people will be lovers of self, lovers of money, proud, arrogant, abusive, disobedient to their parents, ungrateful, unholy, heartless, unappeasable, slanderous, without self-control, brutal, not loving good, treacherous, reckless, swollen with conceit, lovers of pleasure rather than lovers of God, having the appearance of godliness, but denying its power. Avoid such people. For among them are those who creep into households and capture weak women, burdened with sins and led astray by various passions, always learning and never able to arrive at a knowledge of the truth. Just as Jannes and Jambres opposed Moses, so these men also oppose the truth, men corrupted in mind and disqualified regarding the faith. But they will not get very far, for their folly will be plain to all, as was that of those two men (2 Tim. 3:1-9).

Paul's long list of things going wrong in society remains unchanged today. It is the same list that any godly church leader would give you if asked. That's because the nature of sin remains unchanged, and it will remain so until Jesus's return.

In the next verse, however, Paul offered a contrast. "You, however, have followed my teaching, my conduct, my aim in life, my faith, my patience, my love, my steadfastness" (2 Tim. 3:10). Those who are transformed in times of evil are the people who follow Jesus' teachings. They refuse to give in to the worldliness around them, instead living wholeheartedly for Christ.

Godly resistance to worldliness is crucial in every generation. Note what David said in Psalm 14:3: "They have all turned aside." You can't turn aside from something unless you first adhered to it. In this verse, David described people who were once faithful but later turned aside from the Lord to follow the ways of the world. In other words, they were once part of the righteous generation.

Paul wanted to prevent this from happening to the Christians under Timothy, a young minister in training. So Paul gave Timothy a specific charge:

> I charge you in the presence of God and of Christ Jesus, who is to judge the living and the dead, and by his appearing and his kingdom: preach the word; be ready in season and out of season; reprove, rebuke, and exhort, with complete patience and teaching. For the time is coming when people will not endure sound teaching, but having itching ears they will accumulate for themselves teachers to suit their own passions, and will turn away from listening to the truth and wander off into myths. As for you, always be sober-minded, endure suffering, do the work of an evangelist, fulfill your ministry (2 Tim. 4:1-5).

Once again, we see the contrast between the wicked and the righteous in a given generation. While the wicked fall further into corruption, the righteous endure sound teaching and adhere to truth. Their teachers remain sober-minded, enduring suffering and evangelizing faithfully, despite the most challenging times.

"TOGETHER" DESCRIBES THE WICKED GENERATION

The corruption of a wicked generation happens as a joint effort, a coming together. "They have all turned aside; *together* they have become corrupt" (Psalm 14:3, my emphasis). This speaks of a communal effort, a discussion, a trend, and even a calamitous party spirit. In short, it's a movement. The essence of "together" in this scenario is summed up in Psalm 2. "The kings of the earth set themselves, and the rulers take counsel together, against the LORD" (PSALM 2:2).

What is the message of this movement? It's a prevailing wind of a false doctrine that soon becomes the cultural norm. These deceptions end up in the realms of education, entertainment, government, and, sadly, sometimes the church. Congregations that allow this spirit in their midst are soon walking, talking, and acting as the world does. Their services are like the entertaining shows the world puts on. In the midst of it all, the gospel goes missing.

Make no mistake, these churches have turned aside. In fact, when David spoke of a corrupt generation, he was speaking of God's people. "Together they have *become* corrupt" (Psalm 14:3, my emphasis). This clearly speaks of people who have fallen away. After all, to *become* something means you weren't that before.

So what does the righteous generation do in the midst of such corruption? They watch over their hearts. As they see others falling away, they are careful not to slip into the same worldly traps. They resolve, "I will watch over my soul. I'm going to guard my heart so that I stay faithful. To do this, I have to call on the Lord. Holy Spirit, I need Your power to keep me in this hour of great temptations."

Such a generation takes seriously Paul's admonition: "Therefore let anyone who thinks that he stands take heed lest he fall" (1 Cor. 10:12). Here is a deep and important warning. We are to take heed to guard our hearts against false teachings, tempting influences, and worldly indoctrination. We have to be especially vigilant to guard against this within the church. A righteous generation cannot allow a watered-down gospel to replace the holy gospel of Christ.

GUARD YOUR HEART

"Obey your leaders and submit to them, for they are keeping watch over your souls, as those who will have to give an account" (Heb. 13:17). We must seek leaders who are faithful to God and His Word, elders who understand the charge God has given them to shepherd our souls. In turn, we must recognize our vital need for pastoral care and protection.

The greatest example of what a shepherd does is found in a very familiar Bible passage. "The LORD is my shepherd; I shall not want. He makes me lie down in green pastures. He leads me beside still waters. He restores my soul. He leads me in paths of righteousness for his name's sake" (Psalm 23:1-3). When we have a Shepherd Who is faithful to lead us in these ways, we gladly follow their direction.

Talk about a countercultural idea, though. Obey a peer? Most people, including many Christians, are determined to live according to their own rebellious truth. They won't tolerate someone telling them not to do certain things. Whether they admit it or not, they have cast off restraints of their choosing.

Such rebellious defiance can be subtle. For instance, it plagues the so-called prosperity movement that holds influence over so many Christians. Most prosperity churches gather together around false teachings that ride on the winds of fleshly doctrines. Believers are taught they can claim anything they want, that they can create their own reality. Pastors bless the people's aspirations to have every material good they desire and grasp higher positions in the world.

This heresy teaches people that God is Someone they can use. Their leaders don't use that language; but as parishioners leave their services, their thoughts aren't about what the Lord wants of their lives but rather the material benefits they can gain from God. In short, they are not God's; God is theirs.

THE DIFFERENCE OF SUCCESS OF A RIGHTEOUS GENERATION

To the righteous, success is godly obedience, reverence, and adherence to God's Word, receiving from the Holy Spirit all that we need through prayer. This is how a righteous generation lives out success. It means we run from all false teaching. We flee those who tell us life is meant to be only comfort and ease.

We also flee performance-oriented churches. These are churches that are more concerned about how well things go onstage than about the condition of your heart. They don't preach against sin; instead, they just give helpful life tips. The pastors don't contend with people getting drunk, high, or sleeping around; they want to draw the biggest crowds possible, so they water down their sermons. The subtle message you take away from their services is, "Put on a good show."

The righteous generation runs from these churches. They also flee the progressive movement that's infiltrating the church. This movement is just a rehashing of the liberal church, which denies basic Christian doctrines, such as the virgin birth, the second coming, Heaven and Hell, Christ's resurrection, and the infallibility of Scripture. Their attitude is,

"The church needs to move away from its old-school, fire-and-brimstone message. It also needs to replace the ancient hymns about sin and salvation. Our God is One of love, Who would never judge anyone. He understands the world we live in, that people have urges they need to meet. What the world needs most is for everyone to come together in love."

These so-called gospels are wellsprings of deception. The righteous generation needs to seek out churches led by humble, godly, Bible-preaching pastors who stand strong on God's Word and contend with evil. These pastors don't have to be charismatic or super-gifted. They only have to be faithful.

CALLING ON THE NAME OF THE LORD

Despite all the corruption, wickedness, and rejection of God laid out in Psalm 14:1-4, none of these are problems that the Lord can't solve. He changes corrupt hearts. What keeps the righteous from sliding into the company of the wicked is faithfulness to call on God's name. David might easily have turned aside and become corrupt like so many others. In Psalm 13, he wrote of feeling forgotten and abandoned by God. When his prayers weren't answered, he wrote, "How long must I take counsel in my soul and have sorrow in my heart all the day? How long shall my enemy be exalted over me?" (Psalm 13:2). At any time, David could have thrown off his history with the Lord and said, "This just doesn't work anymore."

Instead, as the next verse reveals, David called on the Lord. "Consider and answer me, O LORD my God; light up my eyes, lest I sleep the sleep of death" (Psalm 13:3). In the midst of all the corruption around him, David kept turning to God. He declared two verses later, "But I have trusted in your steadfast love" (Psalm 13:5).

By contrast, in Psalm 14, we see an entire generation that backslid and refused to call on God's name. That is the key difference between the generations of the wicked and the righteous. The difference is not moral fortitude or any other character quality; the difference is the act of calling on God. When you call on the name of the Lord, you gain spiritual discernment. This is the ability to look at the world and recognize, "That is evil, and that is good." "Those who have their powers of discernment trained by constant practice to distinguish good from evil" (Heb. 5:14). We have to keep our discernment sharp to know whether we're still focused on the things of God. In this way, discernment helps us guard our hearts.

A SPIRITUAL EFFECT ON THE WICKED

Verse five describes the effect we have on the wicked generation. "There they are in great terror, for God is with the generation of the righteous" (Psalm 14:5). This verse shifts the whole focus of the psalm. It moves from describing how bad things are to showing an alternative. This alternative is a counterculture established by the vibrant lives of a holy remnant. As the wicked behold God's righteousness in His people, they tremble. They recognize that good is possible in times of evil. They realize deep in their hearts that they have made the wrong choice for their lives; they don't have to live abominably in perverseness and corruption. God has made a good way available to them, and they have rejected it.

Human nature is inherently wicked; and it is devastating and disturbing when we realize how hopelessly lost we are, refusing to live as we know we've been created to live. An even greater shock comes when we see that God has looked down on corrupt humankind and, rather than destroy us, has mercifully shown us a way to life. This awesome contrast between God's loving kindness and our chosen sin is revealed, and it sends us to our knees.

The God of mercy and grace says to a corrupt generation, "I'm calling you out of your sin. I'm raising up a holy people, a righteous generation that will contend with evil, confront falsehood, and speak truth in love." This remnant responds by loving truth and living the gospel, fully embracing "that while we were still sinners, Christ died for us" (Rom. 5:8).

The transformation that takes place in us confuses the wicked generation. It also terrifies them because they realize they have to choose between two paths. "Choose this day whom you will serve . . . But as for me and my house, we will serve the Lord" (Josh. 24:15). Do not be mistaken: The world is watching you. As you stand amidst a culture that increasingly departs from God's ways, you are seen for how you actively love others. This terrifies the watching world because they live totally contrary to that. When they see you stand firmly amidst all chaos with a quiet and confident spirit, they realize how confused they are about a world in disarray. As you endure a difficult season, they see you steadied by a righteous faith; and they realize it comes from beyond your own power. They watch you face wave after wave of chaos and stand unmovable. They see that you're unwilling to abandon what you know and that you're resistant to the cultural norm of rejecting God. The life of Christ in you shines as a light into darkness. You are His salt in the midst of decay.

Simply put, your faithfulness is a testimony against the world, and it causes terror. The worldly realize, "It's truly possible for someone to live an honest life in this mess"; and this brings conviction upon them. They realize a choice has to be made.

TEMPTED TO FEAR ABOUT THE FUTURE

People often ask me, "Are things going to get worse?" As darkness increases, we may be frightened for our children and grandchildren. I see Psalm 14 addressing this head on. We shouldn't be frightened of the world; the world is actually frightened of us. Through the actions of a righteous generation, the world's evil is confronted with the terrifying righteousness of God.

Think about this. The world sees a generation freed from captivity to sin. It sees God's righteous ones turning back darkness by faithfully standing on His Word. Wickedness that once ran rampant and unhindered is limited and disarmed by the righteousness that God has placed within His people. The world can no longer suppress the truth it has tried to disbelieve. God's grace toward sinners makes the difference, as a righteous generation demonstrates the freedom that comes with salvation. People who were once addicted, downtrodden, and despairing now have power against the prevailing winds of the world. They walk in an abundant life no matter what happens around them.

Psalm 14 concludes on such a note. "Oh, that salvation for Israel would come out of Zion! When the Lord restores the fortunes of his people, let Jacob rejoice, let Israel be glad" (Psalm 14:7). The Hebrew root of the phrase "restores the fortunes" means to bring out of captivity. This liberty does not come through political ramifications. It comes through a people who trust wholly in God, and they find faith by calling on His name. You see, the ultimate cry of the righteous is not to become good or to stop doing bad. The cry is for salvation that comes from outside of ourselves. God's grace comes to us not by human power or might but by His Spirit of grace.

A HOLY RESTORATION THAT LEADS TO GLADNESS

Are you troubled over the condition of the world around you? Turn your focus onto what God wants to do and what He wants you to become. Are you more preoccupied with the problems in your country or with the Lord's terrifying holiness? God is raising up a righteous generation, and you can glorify Him by being part of it. If you want your life to make an impact on the world, make the following your prayer:

"Lord, make of me what I cannot make of myself. I can't maintain a faith on my own. Without You, I have no understanding. Thank You, Jesus, for saving me and for putting in me this hunger for You. Fill me with Your presence to live a righteous life. Keep me from falling into the corruption of this world and from turning aside from You. I call on Your name, putting everything into Your hands, including my wellbeing in a darkened time. Enable me to be a part of Your righteous generation. With You, I can worship with gladness of heart." Amen.

CHAPTER THREE

Psalm 15
Who Can Stand Before a Holy God?

1 O Lord, who shall sojourn in your tent?
  Who shall dwell on your holy hill?
2 He who walks blamelessly and does what is right
  and speaks truth in his heart;
3 who does not slander with his tongue
  and does no evil to his neighbor,
  nor takes up a reproach against his friend;
4 in whose eyes a vile person is despised,
  but who honors those who fear the Lord;
  who swears to his own hurt and does not change;
5 who does not put out his money at interest
  and does not take a bribe against the innocent.
He who does these things shall never be moved.

THE ENDING PHRASE OF THIS Psalm, "shall never be moved," also translates as "shall not be shaken" (NIV). Both images suggest amazing strength. For a psalm that is only five verses long, the message contained here carries a power that's both challenging and reassuring to us as Christians.

The first thing we see in this Psalm is movement, specifically an image of traveling ("who shall sojourn" [Psalm 15:1]). David wrote the Psalm, and his language here speaks of more than travel to a destination. To sojourn conveys a purpose behind the journey. In this case, it is a journey toward the Lord's presence: "Who shall dwell on your holy hill?" (Psalm 15:1). David's question here came from a place of deep reverence and longing. He was asking, "Who gets to enter God's holy presence?"

The culture today is utterly irreverent about God's holy Word, and this attitude has seeped into the Christian culture. As a minister, I grieve over churchgoers who have a casual attitude about entering God's presence. It's worse when ministers craft their sermons as self-help messages, with a few Bible verses included only to back up their theme. Jesus may be mentioned, but He isn't made central to the worship service.

Scenarios like these are what pass today for dwelling in the Lord's presence, but nothing about them reflects the reality of His holiness. Sadly, a lot of pastors have become chaplains of a self-help movement rather than shepherds over faithful people who hunger to sojourn to the Lord's holy hill where they may dwell in His presence.

OVERESTIMATING SELF, UNDERESTIMATING THE HOLINESS OF GOD

It's understandable for people to want to know their worth and value. It is tragic, however, to hear God's Word preached as an emotion-based psychological manual rather than as the truth-based Word that is the living Christ. The message we hear from the self-help pulpit is, "You're good just the way you are. You don't need to change anything. God is your Friend."

The higher we see ourselves, however, the lower we see God. When we prioritize our desires over Him, we're looking through the wrong end of the telescope. Have you ever peered into a telescope the wrong way? If so, the vast image you searched for appeared tiny. That is the effect on our view of God when we center our lives on our desires rather than on Him. Reality becomes distorted. God is immense, beyond measure, and beyond our understanding; and the scope of His existence is limitless. Only when we align our vision with His Word does our view of Him grow appropriately larger. To see Him as He truly is (to the extent that we can), far above all we can think or imagine, requires that He comes first in all we think and do.

This, in part, is what it means to sojourn to His holy hill to enter His presence. It is to act on our desire to see Him appropriately as glorious, holy, omnipotent, and omnipresent. So, in practical terms, how does this happen?

WHO GETS TO ENTER GOD'S PRESENCE?

The proper way to address David's question is to begin with the first commandment. "You shall have no other gods before me" (Exod. 20:3). When our own desires are our first priority, where does that place God? By losing sight of His rightful place over all things, we violate His first commandment to us.

Most worship services in the self-help church are a mix of the holy and the self. They draw on cultural elements like entertaining songs and well-produced videos to engage emotions rather than to stir reverence. The sermons are shaped to speak to people's egos, attractive messages meant to draw them back to church instead of challenging them to seek a deeper walk with Christ.

God is holy; and to be in His presence demands holiness and proper reverence. "But as he who called you is holy, you also be holy in all your conduct" (1 Peter 1:15). This speaks of a people set apart for God's holy purposes. That is the point of the sojourn David pictures: to seek God's presence, where we are made holy for His calling on our lives.

How recently did you hear a sermon about God fulfilling your destiny or your wildest dreams? By contrast, when was the last time you heard a message about setting aside your desires to serve Jesus? Self-fulfillment won't save anyone. On the contrary, the elevation of self hinders the humility required to recognize our brokenness as fallen sinners. We need a Savior Who is right with God, clean, pure, and worthy in Himself.

This culture grates against any need for a Savior, claiming we only need to feel good enough about ourselves so that the thought of a Savior wouldn't occur to us. This message is one of entitlement, assuming we're owed a self-fulfilled life. If we life by the self-help gospel, however, we end up shifting the meaning of Christ's gospel. The focus of our calling becomes about successful living instead of sanctified living. The message at its core is, "Believe in yourself," rather than, "Believe in Jesus."

At one time in the church, it was common to hear Christians claim, "I'm a King's kid." This wasn't a bad focus, necessarily, but I always thought it needed a slight shift. Instead of claiming to be a child of the King, a better focus would be, "Behold the King of kings."

To sojourn to God's holy hill isn't about the need to be fulfilled but the need to be changed and transformed. We need God to do a work in us that we can't do on our own. If we think we're fine and don't need transformation, if we think we can achieve all that the Lord has designed for us by working on our self-esteem, we're heading in the opposite direction of His holy hill. We need to stop quoting only those Bible passages that promise possibility and begin to embrace the passages that rebuke and correct as well. The message a vast number of struggling Christians needs to hear right now isn't "be fulfilled" but "be righteous."

AN AWARENESS OF OUR FALLEN NATURE

While David was curious about who gets to enter God's holy presence, he was acutely aware of his own fallenness. He was on a heartrending search for truth, and he posed his question within a particular context. In the preceding Psalm, he stated, "There is none who does good, not even one" (Psalm 14:3). In that Psalm, he wrote about the corruption of the human heart and our capability to commit terrible abominations. He took this further by stating that some people collude to do evil. "They have all turned aside; together they have become corrupt" (Psalm 14:3).

As I wrote in the previous chapter, Paul quoted Psalm 14 in his epistle to the Romans: "As it is written: 'None is righteous, no, not one; no one understands; no one seeks for God. All have turned aside; together they have become worthless; no one does good, not even one" (Rom. 3:10-12). If this was so, David wondered, then who gets to sojourn to God's holy hill? If none are righteous, who can possibly enter the Lord's righteous presence?

I believe the Holy Spirit led the compilers of the psalter to place Psalm 15 strategically after Psalm 14. David had humankind's prevailing wickedness in mind when he asked who gets to enter God's holy presence. Then, in the Psalm that followed, he answered his own question. "He who walks blamelessly and does what is right and speaks truth in his heart" (Psalm 15:2).

On one hand, this answer makes perfect sense. We certainly can't enter and enjoy God's presence if we lead lives of wickedness. It is impossible to be in God's presence while committing abominable things; His presence requires us to reckon with our evil deeds. By repenting, we resolve to do what David prescribed—that is, to walk blamelessly, do right and speak truth in our heart. This resonates with the redemption we have been given; and we agree, "Yes, I'm to speak the truth and not slander my neighbor. If I do these things, I'll be righteous. Then I can enter the Lord's presence."

The problem is, no one does these things—perfectly, regularly, or at all. Even if someone does them consistently, Paul pointed out, "Yet we know that a person is not justified by works of the law but through faith in Jesus Christ, so we also have believed in Christ Jesus, in order to be justified by faith in Christ and not by works of the law, because by works of the law no one will be justified" (Gal. 2:16). Simply put, no one earns the right to come into God's presence by their own power, no matter how many good works they do.

HOW CAN ANYONE COME NEAR TO GOD?

I believe David had a foreshadowing of the gospel as Paul expressed it in Ephesians 4. Paul's message to the church in Ephesus parallels Psalm 14 almost exactly with the added, redeeming lens of Christ. He wrote, "Now this I say and testify in the Lord, that you must no longer walk as the Gentiles do, in the futility of their minds. They are darkened in their understanding, alienated from the life of God because of the ignorance that is in them, due to their hardness of heart. They have become callous and have given themselves up to sensuality, greedy to practice every kind of impurity" (Eph. 4:17-19).

Paul was obviously talking about the ungodly, and his words echo those of Psalm 14. "The fool says in his heart, 'There is no God.' They are corrupt, they do abominable deeds; there is none who does good" (Psalm 14:1). As we skip ahead in Ephesians 4, we see what David foresaw of how we might live:

> Therefore, having put away falsehood, let each one of you speak the truth with his neighbor, for we are members one of another. Be angry and do not sin; do not let the sun go down on your anger, and give no opportunity to the devil. Let the thief no longer steal, but rather let him labor, doing honest work with his own hands, so that he may have something to share with anyone in need. Let no corrupting talk come out of your mouths, but only such as is good for building up, as fits the occasion, that it may give grace to those who hear. And do not grieve the Holy Spirit of God, by whom you were sealed for the day of redemption. Let all bitterness and wrath and anger and clamor and slander be put away from you, along with all malice (Eph. 4:25-31).

Here is a vision of a redeemed people as seen through the finished work of Christ. Paul was showing the Ephesians how to have peace with God, walk with Him, and know His presence in their lives, resulting in abundant joy. Note how close his prescription was to David's. These were all works, good behavior, and deeds that Paul instructed the Ephesians to do. They reflect David's prescription to become "he who walks blamelessly and does what is right and speaks truth in his heart; who does not slander with his tongue and does no evil to his neighbor, nor takes up a reproach against his friend" (Psalm 15:2-3).

So if our own good works are as filthy rags in God's sight, how does someone become righteous and able to enter God's presence? The apostle Paul's testimony reveals how.

THE WORST SINNER OF ALL

Paul wrote, "The saying is trustworthy and deserving of full acceptance, that Christ Jesus came into the world to save sinners, of whom I am the foremost" (1 Tim. 1:15). How could Paul be that awful of a sinner when he claimed to be the most upright of all Jews? "Though I myself have reason for confidence in the flesh also. If anyone else thinks he has reason for confidence in the flesh, I have more: circumcised on the eighth day, of the people of Israel, of the tribe of Benjamin, a Hebrew of Hebrews; as to the law, a Pharisee; as to zeal, a persecutor of the church; as to righteousness under the law, blameless" (Phil. 3:4-6).

The reason Paul called himself the foremost of sinners wasn't because he was a murderer or adulterer. It was because he'd been confident in his own righteousness, believing that it qualified him for salvation and a place in God's presence. Once he saw the work of Christ, however, Paul despised his own righteousness, recognizing it as filthy rags in comparison. He stated this profoundly and powerfully to the Philippians.

> Indeed, I count everything as loss because of the surpassing worth of knowing Christ Jesus my Lord. For his sake I have suffered the loss of all things and count them as rubbish, in order that I may gain Christ and be found in him, not having a righteousness of my own that comes from the law, but that which comes through faith in Christ, the righteousness from God that depends on faith—that I may know him and the power of his resurrection, and may share his sufferings, becoming

like him in his death, that by any means possible I may attain the resurrection from the dead (Phil. 3:8-11).

In these passages, Paul described the transformation that David sought so earnestly. He revealed how people go from corrupt lives to putting off unrighteousness and becoming loving, tender, peacemaking people. That is how Paul described the Ephesians, who clearly had found a place in God's presence. Paul laid out key to their transformation: "But that is not the way you learned Christ!—assuming that you have heard about him and were taught in him, as the truth is in Jesus, to put off your old self, which belongs to your former manner of life and is corrupt through deceitful desires, and *to be renewed in the spirit of your minds, and to put on the new self, created after the likeness of God in true righteousness and holiness*" (Eph. 4:20-24, my emphasis).

First, Paul pointed out that the Ephesians didn't learn Christ through lawlessness—that is, by giving in to sin and erroneously saying, "God accepts me just the way I am. I could live any kind of sinful life that I want, and God will still allow me to dwell in His presence." Paul also pointed out that the Ephesians didn't learn Christ through their own self-righteousness or self-effort, first failing and then trying harder only to fail again. Paul declared, "There is a better way."

That way is revealed in Paul's short but revealing phrase in Ephesians 4: "the truth is in Jesus" (Eph. 4:21). This means more than simply Jesus is the embodiment of truth. It suggests that when we study Scripture, allowing ourselves to be impacted thoroughly by God's Word, we aren't just learning about Jesus and doctrine; we are learning *because we are in Him*. By immersing ourselves in God's Word, we are immersed in Jesus, surrounded by Him, covered by Him, and bathed in Him. When we are in

His Word, our heart is being not just taught but transformed; by being in Him, we are experiencing truth.

Abiding in Him, covered in His righteousness, we are able, as Paul instructs the Ephesians, to put off our old self and be renewed in our minds. We are also able to "put on the new self, created after the likeness of God in true righteousness and holiness" (Eph. 4:24). All of this is empowered by the Holy Spirit. We need God's grace to put off our old self, the self of corrupt, deceitful desires, yet we need Him equally in order to put on us the new self, which verse twenty-four says is created by God. This new self cannot be of our own making. Only the mind of Christ within us can say, "I will no longer live in the way of Psalm 14. I'm going to be a Psalm 15 follower of Jesus."

We can't just "fake it till we make it." God is the creator of all new things, and we need Him to do the work of making us new.

AS GOD CREATES THE NEW SELF IN US

God is the Author of the heavens and the earth, of light and darkness, of the ocean and the land, of man and woman. He created humankind by breathing into Adam and Eve; and the same power that created light by commanding, "'Let there be light'" (Gen. 1:3), also creates the new self in us. What, exactly, is the new self that God creates in us? Paul says it is "The likeness of God in true righteousness and holiness" (Eph. 4:24). The righteousness that God puts in us is nothing like our manufactured righteousness, which fails and falls short of His commands. His righteousness empowers us to do everything Paul instructed in this chapter.

Maybe you've had a problem with gossip or slander in the past. God not only created a new heart in you to save you, which is called justification;

He has also created in you a new way of thinking of others that is loving rather than resentful or judging. This is called sanctification. His Spirit in us deals with our sin issues one by one, with truth upon truth, correcting our heart and leading us in the way of true righteousness.

God alone can create a holiness that is acceptable to Him. So would you rather have a core identity that's created by God or a self-built sense of esteem? A righteousness of our own making gets us nowhere when it comes to being right with God and entering His presence. Being told we're brilliant and wonderful are nice things to hear, but we can be each of those things and never have God's presence in our life. We need something that is beyond our own self-making, and that is the imputed righteousness of Christ.

The miracle of this is that God not only makes us acceptable to Him; He transforms us fully, empowering us to leave behind a life of sinful corruption and enter a new life of doing right in all things. We love our neighbors because God enables us to love them, and we speak truth because we live in Him who is the truth.

A QUESTION AND A PROMISE

David framed Psalm 15 with the idea of dwelling with God. What a glorious conclusion he brings us to in the final verse. Because of Jesus, even the most broken among us can dwell in the house of the Lord forever. I thank God that He gives us the ability to walk in abundant life, exchanging our old, corrupt self with a new self that lives in Him. Yes, we are the ones who get to sojourn to the Lord's holy hill, thanks to the cleansing blood of Jesus, Who took away our sin on the cross. He is our Forerunner into the place of holiness by His perfect sacrifice and by resurrecting us into His life. Every day, He is creating our new self and transforming us into His righteous image.

Friend, you are no longer a Psalm 14 person. You are a Psalm 15 person because Jesus made it possible.

CHAPTER FOUR

Psalm 16
The Preservation of the Saints

1 Preserve me, O God, for in you I take refuge.
2 I say to the Lord, "You are my Lord;
   I have no good apart from you."
3 As for the saints in the land, they are the excellent ones,
   in whom is all my delight.
4 The sorrows of those who run after another god shall multiply;
   their drink offerings of blood I will not pour out
   or take their names on my lips.
5 The Lord is my chosen portion and my cup;
   you hold my lot.
6 The lines have fallen for me in pleasant places;
   indeed, I have a beautiful inheritance.
7 I bless the Lord who gives me counsel;
   in the night also my heart instructs me.
8 I have set the Lord always before me;
   because he is at my right hand, I shall not be shaken.
9 Therefore my heart is glad, and my whole being rejoices;
   my flesh also dwells secure.

> 10 For you will not abandon my soul to Sheol,
>   or let your holy one see corruption.
> 11 You make known to me the path of life;
>   in your presence there is fullness of joy;
>   at your right hand are pleasures forevermore.

THE HEADING THAT APPEARS ABOVE this Psalm contains the word *miktam*, a Hebrew word that isn't well known and doesn't translate easily. Reputable commentaries say that one aspect of miktam suggests a meaning of "hide or conceal." This doesn't speak of a need for safety, however; miktam is a depth of truth or understanding that isn't immediately apparent. In 1858, the writer James Frame claimed that the presence of this one word indicated "a depth of doctrinal or spiritual import that neither the writer (of the Psalm) nor any of his contemporaries had fathomed."[2]

In other words, *miktam* has a prophetic dimension. It speaks of revelations that aren't arrived at by human wisdom. The writer Andrew Bonar said the presence of miktam here suggests that Psalm 16 should be hung on a wall, inscribed on a pillar, or chiseled in stone to commemorate a victory. The victory was that something important had been preserved, and the power that did this preserving was the Holy Spirit. David heralded this in the opening sentence, "Preserve me, O God, for in you I take refuge" (Psalm 16:1).

In this one sentence, David also states the subject of his psalm: God's power to keep and preserve His people. Specifically, what the psalm commemorated was a defeat of an enemy, and that enemy was death.

---

[2] Charles Haddon Spurgeon, *The Treasury of David: Psalm Chapters 1-16* (Independently Published, 2017).

Obviously, that's a unique kind of victory, and it comes only through salvation in Christ. Indeed, Psalm 16 prophesied all that the Messiah was going to do for humankind.

SIX WONDERFUL PROMISES THAT SPEAK OF UNPARALLELED TRANSFORMATION

If we accept by faith the six promises in Psalm 16, then according to David, they will keep us blessed, encouraged, and protected from defeat, despair, and the entrapment of sin. All of these promises are contained in David's opening word, "Preserve" (Psalm 16:1). This speaks of God's keeping power. Another way to read the verse is, "Keep me, O God."

One of the great truths of Scripture is that we are kept by the holy promises of God. That which the Lord speaks, He keeps; and He has spoken into existence our peace and salvation. He has also spoken into existence our communion with Him and a life in community, among every other blessing. These are precious, powerful, and preserving promises.

To better understand the relevant aspects of "preserve," let's break down its meaning in verse one. The prefix "pre" means "before" or "preceding." This indicates that God is *already serving*. Therefore, even before we make a request to Him, He has spoken His promises into existence. By faith, we are to enter into those existing promises. In short, He has already provided the power to keep or preserve us, even before we sense we need it. So what is He keeping us from, exactly? First, He keeps us from wickedness and evil and second, from death and Hell.

This word "preserve" has several dimensions. It can mean to preserve *from* something or to preserve *for* something. God is not only keeping us from evil but is also moving us forward to blessings, as He is engaged in our inheritance.

In the formal study of Scripture, there is a scholarly practice called "first mention" or "first use." This refers to the significance of a word or phrase being mentioned for the first time. Its initial use is meant to lay a foundation for every use of the word that follows. In the case of "preserve," it is first mentioned in Genesis, when God called Adam and Eve to be keepers of the garden or to tend it.

This also was David's primary meaning when he asked God to preserve him in Psalm 16. His request wasn't a defensive stance, seeking protection from evil. Rather, he was asking God to cultivate the garden of his life, meaning all things that were dear to him—his family, his calling, his mission, his ministry, and his responsibility to the nation. David was acknowledging that God had the power to preserve everything about his life. He desired God's ongoing tending of his heart to keep the promise of preservation alive.

"Preserve" also translates as the act of a watchman who protectively oversees lives and sends warnings. Some of Israel's prophets were tasked to be watchmen on their cities' walls. If they failed to warn when the enemy approached, they were held accountable, paying the price with their own lives for not guarding the lives of the people. The same was held true for royal bodyguards. If they let down their guard so that the king or the royal family was left vulnerable, they, too, paid with their lives.

This is the kind of preserving, keeping, and guarding that God does in our lives. He promises, "I won't let down my guard over you. I won't sleep or slumber. You never need to worry because I am watching over you."

One of our greatest needs for preservation today is to be kept from the wickedness of the generation we live in. We need a clean mind and pure heart so that we don't give in to the evil in our midst. We need minds that are fixed on solid doctrine to resist the lukewarmness seeping into the church and avoid succumbing to worldliness. In these ways, David's cry for preservation is absolutely relevant for us today.

THE HEBREW WORD FOR "PRESERVE" USED MANY TIMES THROUGHOUT THE BIBLE

In Genesis 28:15, the Lord promised Jacob, "'Behold, I am with you and will keep you wherever you go, and will bring you back to this land. For I will not leave you until I have done what I have promised you.'" God was promising the patriarch, "I will not only keep you on your journeys, but I'll also bring you home safely to the land of inheritance I have kept for you."

In the New Testament, Peter described God's keeping power in the history of His people:

> If he did not spare the ancient world, but preserved Noah, a herald of righteousness, with seven others, when he brought a flood upon the world of the ungodly; if by turning the cities of Sodom and Gomorrah to ashes he condemned them to extinction, making them an example of what is going to happen to the ungodly; and if he rescued righteous Lot, greatly distressed by the sensual conduct of the wicked (for as that righteous man lived among them day after day, he was tormenting his righteous soul over their lawless deeds that he saw and heard); then the Lord knows how to rescue the godly from trials, and to keep the unrighteous under punishment until the day of judgment" (2 Peter 2:5-9).

As Peter said, if God could keep Noah and Lot in the most disastrous times, He can keep you and me in these perilous days. No one lives in a generation so wicked that the power of God cannot prevail. The Lord looks to preserve His people through *all* things.

Note that God not only keeps His people from harm but that He also keeps judgment for the unrighteous. "The Lord knows how to . . . keep the unrighteous under punishment until the day of judgment" (2 Peter 2:9). God's judgment must begin in our own hearts, as Scripture says; but then it must reach our nation, schools, courts, cities, and churches as part of God's restoration of righteousness in the land.

Jesus used the word "preserve" in His high priestly prayer just before He went to the cross. He prayed, "While I was with them, I *kept* them in your name, which you have given me. I have *guarded* them, and not one of them has been lost except the son of destruction, that the Scripture might be fulfilled" (John 17:12, my emphases). Jesus kept watch over His followers and was faithful to preserve them, just as He does for us today.

His prayer in Matthew 26:42 adds an important dimension to this. It reveals that God's promise to preserve us does not always keep us from suffering: "Again, for the second time, he went away and prayed, 'My Father, if this cannot pass unless I drink it, your will be done.'" Like our Master before us, we will face pain, suffering, and sacrifice; but as was true of Jesus, we have joy and honor in knowing we remain at the center of the Father's will. We may pray, "Lord, keep me from trouble, trials, and tribulations"; but the greater prayer is, "Keep me from falling, Lord, through all of these things. Empower me to endure whatever You have for me; and while I endure, keep me faithful to your calling."

"FOR IN YOU I TAKE REFUGE" (PSALM 16:1).

In this verse, a question is being answered. That question is, "Where do we find hope?" Our hope, as followers of Jesus, does not come from the wisdom of the world. It doesn't come from the brightest theological minds, keen psychological insights, five-year plans for success, or even the strongest moral fortitude. No, we receive all of God's precious promises in one way—by being *in Him*. "For *in you* I take refuge" (Psalm 16:1, my emphasis). When we abide in Him and immerse ourselves in His Word, our hearts and minds are filled with the power of the Holy Spirit. If we choose to lean on our own understanding, we can lose the power of His promises. The promises still stand, of course; but by our choice, we lose their power.

David's first mention of "refuge" in the Psalms appeared in Psalm 2:12: "Blessed are all who take refuge in him." The context for this was the great turbulence David saw taking place in the world. He asked, "Why do the nations rage and the peoples plot in vain?" (Psalm 2:1). As he saw evil rulers plotting against God's righteousness, he advised them to "kiss the Son" (Psalm 2:12). He was telling them, in essence, to repent, revere, and turn to God's Son.

If, as David said, we are blessed by taking refuge in the Lord, then refuge is not a fearful cowering. It is not having to hide because troubles are coming. No, Psalm 5:11 declares that finding refuge is a joyful matter: "But let all who take refuge in you rejoice; let them ever sing for joy, and spread your protection over them, that those who love your name may exult in you." With God's promises, we are able to delight in Him in the midst of any storm. We can even sing with joy. His protection is so powerful that it leaves no room for fear. It not only keeps us from harm but also turns our mourning into dancing and our sorrow into joy.

SIX POWERFUL PROMISES GOD MAKES TO US

God's first promise appears in verse two. It is the promise to keep us in communion. "I say to the Lord, 'You are my Lord; I have no good apart from you'" (Psalm 16:2). The second promise is to keep us in community. "As for the saints in the land, they are the excellent ones, in whom is all my delight" (Psalm 16:3). The third promise is to preserve the "portion," or blessings, that He has chosen for us. "The Lord is my chosen portion and my cup; you hold my lot" (Psalm 16:5).

The fourth promise is to keep us in His counsel. "I bless the Lord who gives me counsel; in the night also my heart instructs me" (Psalm 16:7). The fifth promise is to preserve our confidence. "I have set the Lord always before me; because he is at my right hand, I shall not be shaken" (Psalm 16:8). The sixth promise is to keep us from the corruption or decay of death, indicating Sheol or Hell. "For you will not abandon my soul to Sheol, or let your holy one see corruption" (Psalm 16:10).

I want to begin with the promise of communion in verse two. At first glance, this verse may seem to say there is nothing good about life outside of the Lord. "I say to the Lord, 'You are my Lord; I have no good apart from you'" (Psalm 16:2). The literal text of this verse doesn't translate well into English. Its meaning is closer to this: "None of my blessings are over or above you." In other words, we can be grateful for our spouse, children, and all the blessings of life we delight in; but we don't put them above the Lord.

This corresponds to the first commandment not to put any god or idol before the Lord. The commandment can be read two ways. First, we are not to bring things into God's presence as if they deserve a comparable position. Second, we are not to elevate anything in our hearts above the Lord. God is first, primary, and preeminent in all things; and by acknowledging Him this way in our hearts is to acknowledge His rightful position in all things.

> He is the image of the invisible God, the firstborn of all creation. For by him all things were created, in heaven and on earth, visible and invisible, whether thrones or dominions or rulers or authorities—all things were created through him and for him. And he is before all things, and in him all things hold together. And he is the head of the body, the church. He is the beginning, the firstborn from the dead, that in everything he might be preeminent (Col. 1:15-18).

I thank God for my wife, my children, my nine grandchildren, and my calling in ministry; yet all of these amazing blessings are not just *from* the Lord but are *in Him*. I delight in His many wonderful gifts, but none compete with my affection for and honor of the Lord.

TWO DIMENSIONS OF THE LORD'S CHARACTER

In verse one, David addressed the Lord as "God"—or the Hebrew word *El*—invoking His omnipotence. In verse two, David's calling on God as "Lord" is actually a name, Yahweh. This is a more personal address because it isn't a title or description. Also in verse two, David uses "Lord" again, this time translated from the name Adonia. The name conveys God as Ruler over all things. Altogether, these names signal that God is all-powerful in His rule yet that He rules in a personal way. This presents a picture of the Lord's personal, keeping power over us. He is where our salvation comes from, and we are able to cherish and enjoy that incomparable gift through our communion with Him.

Second is God's promise to preserve us in community. "As for the saints in the land, they are the excellent ones, in whom is all my delight" (Psalm 16:3). David switched gears quickly here, shifting his focus from the Lord to His people. He seemed to understand Christ's Great Commandment before it was spoken centuries later: that we are to "love the Lord . . . with all [our] heart . . . soul . . . mind and . . . strength" and also to "love [our] neighbor as [ourself]" (Mark 12:30-31). On the heels of his robust desire to be in communion with Yahweh, David also desired to be in intimate community—to love his brothers and sisters deeply and to receive their love as well.

Even for those of us who have deep relationships with our brothers and sisters, community is more crucial than we may think. On a recent episode of my podcast, I interviewed a young man who had written an article about a provocative idea, "You Need More Than God." I told him I respectfully disagreed; but as I reflected on his topic, I saw what he intended. Often in the church, we have a romanticized idea of, "It's just me and Jesus. I don't need anything else." I don't denounce that statement, but Jesus does call us to things beyond only communing with Him. One of those is community. We need fellowship, for one, because we are all members of Christ's body. Therefore, to miss out on community is to miss out on an important aspect of fellowship with Him. To paraphrase Paul, the eye can't say to the hand or foot, "I don't need you" (1 Cor. 12:15).

I recall a lesson I learned about this when I read about the life of a great Christian writer I had always admired. He was a pastor, but he never spent time with his parishioners because he continually shut himself for prayer and study of the Scriptures. Those are necessary pursuits, but the pastor did this to the utter exclusion of his community. He was never there for his people. It's true that we need God more than anyone or anything else, but we need each other as well; Scripture makes clear that our lives are incomplete without community. How can we honor Jesus' commandment to love our neighbor as ourselves if we don't believe we're necessary to each other's lives?

There are roughly fifty biblical references to "one another," with commands to love, honor, esteem, serve, pray for, and minister to each other. From the very beginning of creation, we were meant to be in close fellowship. "Then the Lord God said, 'It is not good that the man should be alone; I will make him a helper fit for him'" (Gen. 2:18). This is a profound truth; we simply are not meant to do life alone.

The promise of community is deeply connected to the next promise: "The sorrows of those who run after another god shall multiply; their drink offerings of blood I will not pour out or take their names on my lips" (Psalm 16:4). This verse is the negative image of verse three. We're not only called to fellowship with hearts knit together in a holy bond, but we're also called to flee community that is wicked. It's not possible to leave the world in order to escape the company of blatant sin; but we can avoid fellowship with people who are drunkards, lascivious, and double-minded hypocrites who keep one foot in the world while claiming to follow Jesus. "Do not be unequally yoked with unbelievers. For what partnership has righteousness with lawlessness? Or what fellowship has light with darkness?" (2 Cor. 6:14).

According to David, those who live an immoral life of mixture multiply their sorrows. They think that the pursuit of money or an adulterous affair will reduce their sorrows, but those things end up having the opposite effect. David determined, "Their drink offerings of blood I will not pour out or take their names on my lips" (Psalm 16:4). This is powerful imagery, with the reference to "blood offering" relevant to our day through the murder of millions of unborn children. The blood sacrifices of abortion are offered before idols of convenience, avoidance, and hardship.

David would have no part in the schemes of those who plot such wickedness. He prayed for God to preserve him against the tide of evil. His prayer here takes us back to the very opening of the psalter, where he wrote, "Blessed is the man who walks not in the counsel of the wicked, nor stands in the way of sinners, nor sits in the seat of scoffers; but his delight is in the law of the Lord, and on his law he meditates day and night" (Psalm 1:1-2).

PSALM 16 SPEAKS OF GOD'S PLANS FOR OUR LIVES

What did David have in mind when he wrote, "The Lord is my chosen portion and my cup; you hold my lot" (Psalm 16:5)? In this short verse, David referred to three physical objects that describe the Lord's keeping power in our lives: portion, cup, and lot. Each describes a different dimension of the way God holds His precious plans for us in His hands.

Let's look first at "chosen portion." David was speaking of God's plans for him, and he desired not to stray from those plans. He was saying, in essence, "Lord, I want only what you desire for me. All of your plans are magnificent, and I don't want to do anything to diminish them."

With the Lord, we don't have to worry about being short-changed by life. Every good and perfect gift, our chosen portion, comes to us through our communion with Him. Like David, we should take care that we don't lose our Divine portion by choosing our own. We may have ambitions for marriage, family, and career; but if we don't make the Lord our portion, centering our life on Him, our ambitions can derail us from His wonderful plans.

Let's be clear, this chosen portion David referred to has to do with our life on earth. He wrote in Psalm 142, "I cry to you, O Lord; I say, 'You are my refuge, my portion in the land of the living'" (Psalm 142:5). We can be thankful that when we're in Heaven; we'll be free from all pain, sorrow, and sin, spending eternity in Jesus' glorious presence. We should be thankful, too, that God has chosen a portion for us in the here and now.

David added that the Lord was his "cup" (Psalm 16:5). The image here is of a heart overflowing with joyful emotions, one that delights in the Lord. You're probably familiar with David's famous reference to a cup in Psalm 23: "My cup overflows. Surely goodness and mercy shall follow me all the days of my life" (Psalm 23:5-6). We can be sure that God's chosen portion for us isn't just sufficient but that it flows outward from our cup and blesses others.

Some prosperity churches preach that God is one cup, our finances are another cup, and our destiny is yet another cup. No, we have one Cup—Christ—and all of life's blessings spring and flow from Him. "'Whoever believes in me, as the Scripture has said, *Out of his heart will flow rivers of living water*'" (John 7:38).

Finally, David said of the Lord, "You hold my lot" (Psalm 16:5). In the Old Testament, a person's lot might refer to prosperity in terms of land or destiny; but here, David declared that Yahweh Himself was his Lot. As much as David loved Israel, his greatest desire was the Lord, not the land. As king, he had a great inheritance in that land; but his delight, cup, and portion were always the Lord. "The lines have fallen for me in pleasant places; indeed, I have a beautiful inheritance" (Psalm 16:6). In other words,

"What has fallen from God's hand to me is overwhelmingly beautiful in my life." We may experience great career advancements and many wonderful material blessings, but our Lot is always the Lord Himself. He is our Possession.

DAVID'S ANSWER FROM AN EARLIER PSALM

"I bless the Lord who gives me counsel; in the night also my heart instructs me" (Psalm 16:7). This verse sounds like David's quiet reflection on a blessing, yet its context was one of anguished drama. You may remember David's daily torment in Psalm 13: "How long, O Lord? Will you forget me forever? How long will you hide your face from me? How long must I take counsel in my soul and have sorrow in my heart all the day?" (Psalm 13:1-2).

Gone in Psalm 16 was David's sense of aloneness in his trials. The counsel he so desperately sought from God was now very present. His nights were once filled with torrents of grief and wrenching sorrow: "I am weary with my moaning; every night I flood my bed with tears; I drench my couch with my weeping" (Psalm 6:6). Here in Psalm 16, things had changed. David's nights were blessed with peace through the Lord's intimate instruction. "In the night also my heart instructs me" (Psalm 16:7).

Many of us have seasons when we lie down at night wracked by painful worries, fretting over how our trials will ever be resolved. David answered that a night is coming when the Lord's counsel will become clear. He assured us, "If your heart is troubled, the Lord will instruct it. His counsel brings peace." Not only does the Lord give us precious promises; He gives us counsel in how to obtain and possess them and have the faith to enter them fully.

THE LORD WILL NEVER FORSAKE US

"I have set the Lord always before me; because he is at my right hand, I shall not be shaken" (Psalm 16:8). This is quite a turnaround from David's frame of mind in Psalm 13, where he wrote, "Consider and answer me, O Lord my God . . . lest my enemy say, 'I have prevailed over him,' lest my foes rejoice because I am shaken" (Psalm 13:3-4).

What made the difference for David? It was his determination to "set the Lord always before me." He no longer focused on his enemies and their triumphs. Instead, he fixed his eyes on the Lord. King Asa did this to dramatic effect in the Old Testament. Israel's kingdom was surrounded by millions of enemy soldiers with no possible way to defeat them. Asa should have been shaken to his core at the frightening sight; but he fixed his eyes on the Lord instead of on the enemy, and Israel triumphed.

A beautiful phrase is included in this verse about having the Lord always before us: "He is at my right hand" (Psalm 16:8). When we know that the Lord stands beside us, as King Asa surely knew, we won't be shaken, no matter how powerful the enemy that we face is. We can stand firm knowing that the Lord is at our side.

New Testament writers, including Peter and Paul, saw Jesus in this verse. In fact, they quoted it as they evangelized. When Peter preached to the crowds in Jerusalem at Pentecost, he made clear that David was talking about Jesus in Psalm 16:

> God raised [Christ] up, loosing the pangs of death, because it was not possible for him to be held by it. For David says concerning him, "'I saw the Lord always before me, for he is at my right hand that I may not be shaken; therefore my heart was glad, and my tongue rejoiced; my flesh also will dwell in hope. For you will not abandon my soul to Hades, or let your Holy One see corruption. You have made known to me the paths

of life; you will make me full of gladness with your presence'" (Acts 2:24-28).

Peter told the crowd, in essence, "David said that because Jesus saw the Father at His right hand, Christ would not be shaken."

PSALM 16 KEEPS US FROM CORRUPTION

David wrote, "Therefore my heart is glad, and my whole being rejoices; my flesh also dwells secure. For you will not abandon my soul to Sheol, or let your holy one see corruption" (Psalm 16:9-10). As I mentioned earlier, corruption here doesn't refer just to people's spiritual state or to the acts of self-serving politicians or greedy bankers. It refers to physical death, the decay of the body. The promise David invoked here is that God will keep us from sin, death, and separation from the Lord. This kind of corruption begins as rebellion, when people depart from a holy God and descend into wickedness.

This brings us to the most important part of this Psalm. Everything to this point—communion, community, chosen portion, counsel, and confidence—have pointed to this one aspect of being preserved from corruption. In short, it is about resurrection and eternal life. Every other promise is insufficient if this one is missing.

As David closed Psalm 16 with this passage, he presented it as a prophecy of what God would bring to humankind through the work of the Messiah. I return now to Peter's quote from Psalm 16. *"For you will not abandon my soul to Hades, or let your Holy One see corruption. You have made known to me the paths of life; you will make me full of gladness with your presence'"* (Acts 2:27-28).

Peter wanted the crowd at Pentecost to know that David was still prophesying about Jesus here. He preached:

> "Brothers, I may say to you with confidence about the patriarch David that he both died and was buried, and his tomb is with us to this day. Being therefore a prophet, and knowing that God had sworn with an oath to him that he would set one of his descendants on his throne, he foresaw and spoke about the resurrection of the Christ, that he was not abandoned to Hades, nor did his flesh see corruption. This Jesus God raised up, and of that we all are witnesses. Being therefore exalted at the right hand of God, and having received from the Father the promise of the Holy Spirit, he has poured out this that you yourselves are seeing and hearing. For David did not ascend into the heavens, but he himself says, *'The Lord said to my Lord, "Sit at my right hand, until I make your enemies your footstool"'* (Acts 2:29-35).

According to Peter, Jesus never saw the corruption of death because the Father was faithful to keep Him. He presented Psalm 16 that day as a prophecy of Jesus praying, "Father, keep me in communion with You. Keep me in community with those You have chosen for me to shepherd. Keep me in Your counsel, knowing I only do what You tell me. Keep me in confidence so that I am not shaken as I face the cross. Keep me from the grave, Sheol, for You will not allow me to see corruption."

The Father kept Jesus in every way. Because of His preserving love, "it was not possible for him to be held by (death)" (Acts 2:24).

JESUS OUR FORERUNNER

Hebrews echoes both Peter and David, declaring, "We have this as a sure and steadfast anchor of the soul, a hope that enters into the inner place behind the curtain, where Jesus has gone as a forerunner on our behalf, having become a high priest forever after the order of Melchizedek" (Heb. 6:19-20). Jesus has grafted us into Himself, and He will not abandon us to the corruption of death. In fact, the promises of Psalm 16 are ours in the same way they were David's. You see, Psalm 16 is a psalm of the cross, Christ's saving power, and His resurrection and ascension. His portion, cup, lot, and inheritance are ours; and we are to pray the promises of Psalm 16 in agreement with Him.

The "sure and steadfast anchor" mentioned in Hebrews speaks of Christ's preserving power. He brought us to salvation, and He will keep us saved. He brought to us comfort, peace, and joy; and He will forever keep for us all the pleasures at His right hand. "You make known to me the path of life; in your presence there is fullness of joy; at your right hand are pleasures forevermore" (Psalm 16:11). Through David, Jesus declared that all of these promises are ours for eternity; and He lived each of them Himself. He knew how to get through His trials, saying, "I bless the LORD who gives me counsel; in the night also my heart instructs me" (Psalm 16:7).

In the wilderness, when He was tempted by Satan with the promise of earthly kingdoms, Jesus had already determined, "The Lord is my chosen portion and my cup; you hold my lot" (Psalm 16:5). At Gethsemane, facing great anguish on the night of His betrayal, Jesus could say, "I have set the Lord always before me; because he is at my right hand, I shall not be shaken" (Psalm 16:8). With the Spirit's encouraging power, He pressed forward. "Therefore my heart is glad, and my whole being rejoices; my flesh also dwells secure" (Psalm 16:9).

Each of these promises is ours, through Christ's sacrifice and the empowerment of the Holy Spirit. They help to answer David's question in the previous chapter: "Who shall dwell on your holy hill?" (Psalm 15:1). Jesus assures us, "You are with Me in the holy place. Where My flesh dwells securely, so does yours. I will not let you see corruption. In My presence is eternal joy, with pleasures at My right hand."

So we keep strong by fixing our eyes on our elder Brother, Forerunner, and Savior. His promises to preserve us supply confidence that we stand in a sure place with Him. All of our preservation comes from Him, and we endure and remain faithful by His keeping power. His promises to preserve us never fail or falter.

CHAPTER FIVE

Psalm 17a
A Cry for Justice

1 Hear a just cause, O Lord; attend to my cry!
  Give ear to my prayer from lips free of deceit!
2 From your presence let my vindication come!
  Let your eyes behold the right!
3 You have tried my heart, you have visited me by night,
  you have tested me, and you will find nothing;
  I have purposed that my mouth will not transgress.
4 With regard to the works of man, by the word of your lips
  I have avoided the ways of the violent.
5 My steps have held fast to your paths;
  my feet have not slipped.
6 I call upon you, for you will answer me, O God;
  incline your ear to me; hear my words.
7 Wondrously show your steadfast love,
  O Savior of those who seek refuge
  from their adversaries at your right hand.
8 Keep me as the apple of your eye;
  hide me in the shadow of your wings,

9 from the wicked who do me violence,
   my deadly enemies who surround me.
10 They close their hearts to pity;
   with their mouths they speak arrogantly.
11 They have now surrounded our steps;
   they set their eyes to cast us to the ground.
12 He is like a lion eager to tear,
   as a young lion lurking in ambush.
13 Arise, O Lord! Confront him, subdue him!
   Deliver my soul from the wicked by your sword,
14 from men by your hand, O Lord,
   from men of the world whose portion is in this life.
You fill their womb with treasure;
   they are satisfied with children,
   and they leave their abundance to their infants.
15 As for me, I shall behold your face in righteousness;
   when I awake, I shall be satisfied with your likeness.

THE FOCUS OF THIS CHAPTER is an issue that requires the church to stand up and contend. That issue is the difference between social justice and biblical justice. The topic of social justice has been aflame in our nation in recent years, but it caught fire especially in the 1960s. Society's sense of justice then was different from the kind that David cried out to God in Psalm 17. His cry was rooted in biblical justice.

David demanded justice because he was being falsely accused. His life history makes plain his need for God to enact justice for him. David was under continual bombardment from the evil one, who sought to bring him under condemnation. Indeed, the devil allowed David to be viciously slandered by prominent people he loved and served.

For example, David was a warrior for King Saul, winning crucial battles for him. Yet Saul had spells of depression, some appearing to be demonic attacks; and this endangered David. When Saul fell under these dark clouds, David played his harp to soothe the king's spirit. Even so, as David won more and more battles, Saul grew more and more jealous of him. The king grew especially enraged when the Israelites celebrated David's victories more than his own.

> As they were coming home, when David returned from striking down the Philistine, the women came out of all the cities of Israel, singing and dancing, to meet King Saul, with tambourines, with songs of joy, and with musical instruments. And the women sang to one another as they celebrated, "Saul has struck down his thousands, and David his ten thousands." And Saul was very angry, and this saying displeased him. He said, "They have ascribed to David ten thousands, and to me they have ascribed thousands, and what more can he have but the kingdom?" And Saul eyed David from that day on" (1 Sam. 18:6-9).

Once this happened, Saul didn't just keep an eye on David. He grew so paranoid that he began trying to kill him. After the people lauded David's victories: "The next day a harmful spirit from God rushed upon Saul, and he raved within his house while David was playing the lyre, as he did day by day. Saul had his spear in his hand. And Saul hurled the spear, for he thought, 'I will pin David to the wall.' But David evaded him twice" (1 Sam. 18:10-11).

Saul's threats became so fierce that David had to flee Jerusalem and hide in the wilderness among rocks and in caves. Saul's jealousy was so insane that he killed a group of priests who'd given David some bread when he was on the run. These were all literal attacks, threatening David's very life. There is no comparison between this kind of mortal threat and the harmful accusations we may receive from enemies, but they often share the same goal: to pin their opponent to the wall, stifle their life, and keep them from being what God wants them to be. That is the injustice of libel and slander.

DAVID'S PETITIONS THE COURTS OF HEAVEN FOR JUSTICE AND GOD'S FAVOR

Saul wasn't David's only accuser. After the king's death, David's own son, Absalom, also slandered him. He was infuriated that David hadn't avenged the rape of his sister. So Absalom stood at Jerusalem's city gate and planted doubts about David in the ears of arriving Israelites. These people came to Jerusalem to have their disputes settled, and Absalom used the opportunity to undermine David's authority. He assured the people that their claims were promising but said there was no one present in court to hear them. So he, Absalom, would hear their case and give them justice.

> Absalom would say to him, "See, your claims are good and right, but there is no man designated by the king to hear you." Then Absalom would say, "Oh that I were judge in the land! Then every man with a dispute or cause might come to me, and I would give him justice." And whenever a man came near to pay homage to him, he would put out his hand and take hold of him and kiss him. Thus Absalom did to all of Israel who came

to the king for judgment. So Absalom stole the hearts of the men of Israel (2 Sam. 15:3-6).

What Absalom did was totally against God's laws for His people. In effect, he took justice out of God's appointed ways and substituted a form of worldly justice. Absalom had an ungodly agenda; and when you live an injustice, you can't possibly bring true justice to others.

DAVID'S THIRD TERRIBLE INJUSTICE

The book of 2 Samuel tells us:

> When King David came to Bahurim, there came out a man of the family of the house of Saul, whose name was Shimei, the son of Gera, and as he came he cursed continually. And he threw stones at David and at all the servants of King David, and all the people and all the mighty men were on his right hand and on his left. And Shimei said as he cursed, "Get out, get out, you man of blood, you worthless man! The LORD has avenged on you all the blood of the house of Saul, in whose place you have reigned, and the LORD has given the kingdom into the hand of your son Absalom. See, your evil is on you, for you are a man of blood."
>
> Then Abishai the son of Zeruiah said to the king, "Why should this dead dog curse my lord the king? Let me go over and take off his head." But the king said, "What have I to do with you, you sons of Zeruiah? If he is cursing because the Lord has said to him, 'Curse David,' who then shall say, 'Why have you done so?'" And David said to Abishai and to all his servants, "Behold, my own son seeks my life; how much more now may this Benjaminite! Leave him alone, and let him curse, for the LORD has told him to. It may be that the LORD will look on the wrong

done to me, and that the LORD will repay me with good for his cursing today."

So David and his men went on the road, while Shimei went along on the hillside opposite him and cursed as he went and threw stones at him and flung dust. And the king, and all the people who were with him, arrived weary at the Jordan. And there he refreshed himself (2 Sam. 16:5-14).

Once again, we see David being slandered. Yet as awful as these attacks were, David didn't respond as you or I might. Anyone else might take the matters to their friends, seeking support and a "righteous judgment" in order to feel justified in bitter outrage. David didn't do that. He didn't fight back against the lies, even though they came from Hell.

How is it that in all three of these scenarios David responded mercifully? Where do you go when the words of others deliberately wound you? To whom do you turn when your heart is troubled by false accusations? David didn't produce his own vengeance in any of these situations. Instead, he went directly to the Judge of all men.

David was an expert when it came to being slandered, and the opening verses of Psalm 17 show how he dealt with false accusations: He brought everything into the courtroom of the Judge Most High. David didn't seek to vindicate himself. Instead, he looked to the Maker of all men, the Creator of Heaven and earth, the righteous One Who rules from Heaven. David was basically saying, "I can't solve all the false judgments that men bring against me. I can have one thing for sure, though, and that is my right standing with God. My heart is secure in Him."

Think about that kind of stance. David could have lost his kingdom due to all the falsehoods cast at him. He could have lost his family, reputation, status, and high calling to lead God's people. His trust, however, was firm.

DAVID'S CALL FOR JUSTICE

There are two Hebrew words for the four-word English phrase "a just cause, Lord." The first Hebrew word is *Yahweh*, God's name. The second word means "righteousness." I can picture David making a primal, guttural plea, "God, righteousness!" It's as primal as a baby crying, "Mama, hungry!"—a deep soul-cry of pain. David's cry was, essentially, "God, Abba, Father, help me. Hear my heart and bring justice. Attend to my cry, pay attention, hear my pain!"

I see this psalm as very much a legal case. In the first five verses, David made a claim that he was a righteous witness. In verse two, he spoke of having "lips free of deceit!" (Psalm 17:1). He went on to enumerate all the ways his testimony was trustworthy. Based on this, he cried out to the judge for a righteous decree of his innocence. "From your presence let my vindication come! Let your eyes behold the right!" (Psalm 17:2). In other words, "Judge, pronounce one of us guilty, either my accusers or me. You have tested me, so You know that I stand innocent before You. Pronounce guilt on my accusers!"

These are trial words, and David was looking for a righteous form of justice, which, by definition, is biblical justice. That is different from the cry for social justice we hear today. I believe if David heard what today's cries are all about, he would be astounded and disgusted.

Don't misunderstand, I believe fully in social justice. I believe, however, that true social justice is biblical justice. It is caring for the poor, visiting the imprisoned, caring for the outcast, loving your neighbor, and honoring one another. In short, it is having God's heart for *all* the people around you, not just some of the people.

Biblical justice is love for people without classifications. It doesn't mean caring only for those of your own race, gender, education level, or economic class. We are called to care for all, especially those who are treated unjustly with no one to advocate for them. We are to seek the justice of God's heart, whether that is in a courtroom, a classroom, the media, or any other setting. Our cry is the same as David's: "Yahweh, righteousness!"

SOCIAL JUSTICE WITH A CAPITAL *S* AND A CAPITAL *J*

The social justice movement of the 1960s was born in the halls of academia, and it grew to other areas of influence during the '70s and '80s. Articles were published about an unjust society, and there was a lot of merit to what they stated. The remedy, however, was rooted in a system very close to neo-Marxism, ideas not born in Scripture. The movement drew ideas from the Bible; but it twisted them, much the way cults do, to serve self-driven purposes. It diverted people from pure truth and hoodwinked those who weren't careful in understanding the underpinnings of the doctrine.

As Christians, we believe in social justice but not necessarily the movement that began in academia. Professors touted their studies and research as social science, telling their students these doctrines were proven realities. Those claims, however, weren't based in truth; they were opinion. Yet as students graduated, they took the claims into society, bringing them into the realms of media, education, politics, and the corporate world. In this way, academics' ideas of social justice entered the cultural mainstream.

One of its central claims is that no matter who you are, you are part of a system. I am white; and because society is predominantly white, social justice claims that I'm part of a white supremacist system (supremacy representing the top rung of society's ladder and, by definition, being oppressive). Also, because I'm male, the claim is that I'm part of a misogynistic system that oppresses women. Even if I'm not misogynistic or racist—and God's Word and the Holy Spirit won't allow me to be—I am automatically judged to be guilty as part of the system because I'm a white male.

The remedy that the social justice movement prescribes for me isn't to examine myself for misogyny or racism, then repent and turn to the Holy Spirit Who cleanses me and empowers me to live according to His righteous way. Rather, I'm told my only hope is to make myself anti-racist and that this can only happen as I fight the system. In some extreme views of social justice, the solution is to be against being white or male. In other extremes, it is to be anti-government because that's the system that upholds all oppression. It is also to be against Christianity because that's the predominant form of religion in the US. In short, the answer is to tear down *all* systems because they are presumed to be corrupt without the possibility of redemption. We all have heard the rallying cry in recent years, "Tear it down! Burn it down!"

I'm not saying we shouldn't tear down ungodly divisions of racism or the sin of misogyny. We are called to do that work in the name of Christ. The answer, though, isn't to destroy systems because bad things exist within them. Our answer is that God sees the heart and redeems it; He doesn't have to bring down a whole system because He can change it from the inside out. Jesus said, "First clean the inside of the cup and the plate, that the outside also may be clean" (Matt. 23:26).

Where the culture's message of social justice errs is in saying our situation is hopeless. It claims, "There can be no justice if these systems exist, and therefore there can be no reconciliation. Even if reparations were made, a system still exists; and so does its evil. There is no escape from it. For the rest of our lives, we'll be part of that system. Therefore, it must be burned down completely."

Another problem with the social justice movement is that it says there are many truths, even when these truths conflict with each other. There is your truth; there is my truth; and they are different. You've probably heard people asked by TV hosts and reporters, "Tell us your truth." This idea of many truths is rooted in another academic idea: postmodernism. It claims there isn't one truth but only the truth we each perceive or feel. This, too, is a deconstruction, not only of systems but of truth itself.

A lot of pastors have taken a postmodern approach to the Bible. In these circles, the claim is, "There can be no racial reconciliation as Paul describes it because racism is only understood through social justice" (meaning, the secular culture's definition of social justice). They also preach the postmodern message that there isn't absolute truth, only lived truth. They claim that because certain sins aren't unhealthy, they aren't actually sinful. Meanwhile, if a Christian lives out biblical truth to lead an upright life, they're called patriarchal, misogynistic, and a colonialist. These labels come not just from the world but also from fellow Christians.

TRUE JUSTICE IN PSALM 17

David's psalm helps us to picture justice through God's absolute rule. The foremost cry of David's heart as he sought justice was that he would understand God's heart. This, in a nutshell, is the difference between biblical justice and the social justice movement. Biblical justice looks first to God's heart, beholding His nature and attributes. His justice is rooted in His awesome beauty and righteous power. We find this justice by trusting Him to bring light into darkness as we work hard to see the things of His heart become realities in society.

Biblical justice helped America get free from the horrible practice of slavery. Biblical justice also helped start the public school system in the US, which since has moved away from biblical truth toward social justice's academic ideas. This latter example ought to caution us in the ways true justice can be corrupted. In his cry to the Lord, David knew where true justice was found. "From your presence let my vindication come! Let your eyes behold the right!" (Psalm 17:2).

The prophet Daniel had a powerful vision that echoed David's cry. "I saw in the night visions, and behold, with the clouds of heaven there came one like a son of man, and he came to the Ancient of Days and was presented before him. And to him was given dominion and glory and a kingdom, that all peoples, nations, and languages should serve him; his dominion is an everlasting dominion, which shall not pass away, and his kingdom one that shall not be destroyed" (Dan. 7:13-14). The Ancient of Days in this passage was an Old Testament description of Jesus. He was the one sitting on the throne at the right hand of the Father. To both David and Daniel, Christ's rule was the only true justice.

MERCY TO THOSE WHO FALSELY ACCUSED HIM

David could show mercy because he trusted in the omnipotence of God. He knew that the Lord places a conviction for justice in our hearts, empowering us to preach truth that confronts systems of evil. One way to live true justice is to oppose abortion mills. Another is to say, "Don't falsely accuse others."

Here's an example of how biblical truth counters a false accusation. Say, we view a video of a policeman taking some kind of action, and we make a snap judgment that he acted wrongly. With every such thing we see, we have to investigate further because biblical justice requires that we get to the truth. That includes examining our heart, which may have colored how we interpreted the video. Such justice says, "This officer may indeed be guilty, but let's hear the whole case before passing judgment and protesting in the streets."

David waited to pass judgment even on those who wanted to kill him, including Saul and Absalom. Instead of reacting, he waited on the Lord. Only when he knew God's heart on the matter did he pursue justice so that when he did act, he had the full authority of the Ancient of Days, Who sits on the throne.

Likewise, Daniel gave us a picture of the Lord preparing to deliver righteous judgment. "A stream of fire issued and came out from before him; a thousand thousands served him, and ten thousand times ten thousand stood before him; the court sat in judgment, and the books were opened" (Dan. 7:10). The next two verses describe the Lord's power vanquishing the accusing voices of the enemy who call good evil and evil good. "'I looked then because of the sound of the great words that the horn was speaking. And as I looked, the beast was killed, and its body destroyed and given over to be burned with fire. As for the rest of the beasts, their dominion was taken away, but their lives were prolonged for a season and a time'" (Dan. 7:11-12).

This shows us why we can trust God and look to the Ancient of Days. We have a Judge Who vanquishes lies; and He equips us with truth we can rely on, not ideas built on shifting perceptions and feelings. In Psalm 82, we read another dimension of how God issues judgment.

"God has taken his place in the divine council; in the midst of the gods he holds judgment" (Psalm 82:1). We may think of these "gods" as rulers and authorities who show partiality to uphold evil. Today, some of these entities condemn ministries for helping people out of their sinful behaviors. Such ministries are labeled bigoted and hateful when, in truth, they are living and working the justice of God.

The next few verses speak of God's righteous justice toward the poor and oppressed. "'Give justice to the weak and the fatherless; maintain the right of the afflicted and the destitute. Rescue the weak and the needy; deliver them from the hand of the wicked'" (Psalm 82:3-4). This righteous work has been at the heart of the church since day one. Works of truth and love have stood through generations as God's way of enacting justice for the weak, the needy, and the brokenhearted. By enacting such justice, we contend with its false forms. "You shall not pervert justice" (Deut. 16:19).

With true justice, there is no twisting of words or truth. The same passage in Deuteronomy continues, "You shall not show partiality, and you shall not accept a bribe, for a bribe blinds the eyes of the wise and subverts the cause of the righteous" (Deut. 16:19). We're not to show partiality or favoritism, yet the social justice movement commits both by bypassing both the heart of God and the dignity of the person. For example, it automatically classifies a poor person as a victim. It also automatically classifies a person born into a wealthy family as an oppressor. We all know people who would be called victims by these definitions yet whose lives contradict the label by overcoming obstacles, becoming pillars in their community and sometimes rising to governmental leadership. We also know of wealthy people whose hearts, actions, and finances are dedicated to serving the poor and the oppressed, bringing help to large populations.

In short, biblical justice looks at the heart, not the circumstance, whereas labels lead to perversions of true justice.

Every generation is called to stand up for biblical justice. We are to contend for the faith with the love of Jesus Christ, Who is the Truth. The Ancient of Days, Who sits on the throne, calls justice exactly what it is—justice. As David stated, from His presence comes our vindication, for He alone judges righteously.

CHAPTER SIX

Psalm 17b
A Heart After God

1 Hear a just cause, O Lord; attend to my cry!
   Give ear to my prayer from lips free of deceit!
2 From your presence let my vindication come!
   Let your eyes behold the right!
3 You have tried my heart, you have visited me by night,
   you have tested me, and you will find nothing;
   I have purposed that my mouth will not transgress.
4 With regard to the works of man, by the word of your lips
   I have avoided the ways of the violent.
5 My steps have held fast to your paths;
   my feet have not slipped.
6 I call upon you, for you will answer me, O God;
   incline your ear to me; hear my words.
7 Wondrously show your steadfast love,
   O Savior of those who seek refuge
   from their adversaries at your right hand.
8 Keep me as the apple of your eye;
   hide me in the shadow of your wings,

9 from the wicked who do me violence,
  my deadly enemies who surround me.
10 They close their hearts to pity;
  with their mouths they speak arrogantly.
11 They have now surrounded our steps;
  they set their eyes to cast us to the ground.
12 He is like a lion eager to tear,
  as a young lion lurking in ambush.
13 Arise, O Lord! Confront him, subdue him!
  Deliver my soul from the wicked by your sword,
14 from men by your hand, O Lord,
  from men of the world whose portion is in this life.
You fill their womb with treasure;
  they are satisfied with children,
  and they leave their abundance to their infants.
15 As for me, I shall behold your face in righteousness;
  when I awake, I shall be satisfied with your likeness.

IN THE PREVIOUS CHAPTER, WE studied only the first two verses of Psalm 17. Our focus was the difference between the world's view of social justice and a biblical view of social justice. Talking about these concepts can be confusing, but true justice becomes clear and simple once it's viewed through the gospel.

It took a lot of faith for David to rely on God's way of justice. He cried out to the Lord after being falsely accused and literally losing his kingdom. Word against David spread so fast and far that as he fled Jerusalem, people along the way cursed him and threw rocks at him. When David finally took action against the lies, it was according to God's justice, not his own. Again and again, David refused to take justice into his own hands. In the end, the Lord restored him to the kingdom that was ordained for him.

Any effort to create our own justice, however, leads to a false justice. That's because it can't achieve God's justice. A just heart comes from the Lord, Whose nature is to rescue and redeem us from our unjust ways. As we dive further into Psalm 17, we see the amazing ways that the Lord mercifully enabled us to lead a just life toward others.

We've already seen that in composing Psalm 17, David used legal language. "Hear a just cause," "let my vindication come," "behold the right" (Psalm 17:1-2). The Hebrew word for *vindication* here is "sentence," as in a legal pronouncement. David was declaring, "Let my sentence come. As I stand before the judge, I am confident He will see my innocence and vindicate me from these accusations. The facts of this case will be brought to light!" He trusted God with whatever His final sentence would be because the justice he sought was based on the truth he knew from the Lord's Word and from his relationship with God.

David's legal language in this psalm shows that he was eager to work for his justice. The first work of finding justice, however, is to seek God's righteous way. That work begins by coming before the Lord to hear His heart and to know His nature, character, and desires. That is where we find His agenda in our desire for justice.

THE PHYSICAL NATURE OF GOD'S JUSTICE

David invoked physical attributes as he composed this psalm, and it is clear why. When we're wounded by lies, our cry for justice comes from our physical body being wracked by emotional pain. You see, when our character is lambasted, our emotions go into high alert; and those emotions flood into our body. Our reactions to emotional wounds are as much physical as psychological.

In verse one, David spoke of "lips free of deceit," meaning his own. Two verses later, he said that his "mouth will not transgress." In verse ten, he said of his enemies, "With their mouths they speak arrogantly." The image of the mouth suggests how strongly David felt he had to speak out against the injustices flung against him.

The lips and mouth were just the first in David's list of physical elements. He then spoke of ears. "Give ear to my prayer from lips free of deceit!" (Psalm 17:2). "Incline your ear to me; hear my words" (Psalm 17:6). David made it plain he needed God to hear his cry.

Next, David spoke of eyes. "Let your eyes behold the right!" (Psalm 17:2). He was saying, in essence, "Lord, do you see what's happening here? You alone bear witness to what is right and what isn't. Behold the evil that is being done to me!"

David went on to say of eyes, "Keep me as the apple of your eye" (Psalm 17:8). Some Hebrew scholars translate this verse as "the pupil of your eye," meaning, "Keep me in the very center of your vision." David was saying, in other words, "Lord, keep me in your loving communion. My world is falling apart because of these false allegations. Give me your eyes to see your loving heart toward me." We need to be able to see ourselves as He sees us. This puts our hearts at rest, giving us peace and contentment no matter what our circumstance.

That is important because if we're confused about how God perceives us, we leave ourselves open to the lying voices of the world and may absorb their false accusations. That sends our minds and bodies into turmoil. Our nervous system is engaged, and we tense up.

Our heartbeat increases, and our pupils dilate. We begin to sweat, with headaches and rising blood pressure. A book was written about this mind-body connection, titled *The Body Keeps the Score*. It's a scientific view of how mental and emotional pressures from the world impact our bodies. In short, our physical being absorbs all the stresses that mount on us, causing anxiety and fear and possibly leading to ulcers, growths, and even cancer.

By contrast, when we seek the Lord for how He feels about our situation, something healthy happens in our emotions and within our bodies. We receive peace and calm by understanding just how lovingly we're seen by God. This brings health to our entire being. David understood this centuries before scientists did. It enabled him to declare, "I need God to hear my cry. He will see and understand the unjust situation I'm in."

Verse ten provides a contrast, showing the traits of those who pursue their own ideas of justice. "They close their hearts to pity; with their mouths they speak arrogantly" (Psalm 17:10). Instead of seeking the Lord's view of justice, they trust their own. They don't examine their hearts before God, neglecting to seek how He views them and their situation. Instead, they bring their protest straight to men, bypassing the Lord and engaging in conflicts of flesh which don't achieve God's will.

THE NEXT BODY ELEMENT: FEET

"My steps have held fast to your paths; my feet have not slipped" (Psalm 17:5). David not only testified to his innocence but also declared he was on solid ground by seeking the Lord. In contrast, note what he said about his accusers' steps. "They have now surrounded our steps; they set their eyes to cast us to the ground" (Psalm 17:11). While David was committed to walking in biblical truth and justice, he was surrounded by those who called evil good and good evil. These enemies sought to bring him down.

We are immersed in a similar predicament today. We're surrounded by a culture of lies—media that color facts with bias, politicians who twist truth, and institutions bent on punishing those who seek to live justly. Many Christians are tempted to take justice into their own hands, turning to the strength of politicians or other powers; but David preached otherwise. The reason his feet had not slipped was because his eyes remained fixed on the Lord. He kept his heart malleable to God's shaping hand, and that set his feet on a righteous path. He knew he was walking in the right direction.

This brought David to focus on hands. "Deliver my soul from the wicked by your sword, from men by your hand, O Lord, from men of the world whose portion is in this life" (Psalm 17:13-14). David's dilemma was physical, not just intellectual or emotional. Note the way hands were used against him. Saul literally threw a spear at David. Shimei threw rocks at David, cursing him. We can believe in all the right doctrinal principles, but the attacks that come against us from this world have a physical impact. We feel pain deeply, and out of those feelings come palpable tears in reactions to our wounds.

God designed us this way. We are not meant to be stoics but passionate people. As we absorb the impact of false accusations, the Lord has to heal not only our emotions but also our bodies. He brings deep peace alongside physical rest and comfort. When we turn our eyes to Him, our headaches diminish; when we turn our heart to Him, our blood pressure lowers. In this way, miracles of healing take place, not by Divine intervention but through the physicality of how God created us.

A DYNAMIC CONTRAST BETWEEN THE RIGHTEOUS AND THE UNRIGHTEOUS

For the unrighteous, seeking justice is about taking matters into their own hands without living the truth of biblical justice. Another contrast is how the unrighteous come against those who try to live by biblical justice. Note these contrasts from David, as I have emphasized in italics:

- "Give ear to *my prayer from lips* free of deceit . . . With *their mouths* they speak arrogantly . . . " (Psalm 17:1, 10).
- "Keep me as the apple of *your eye* . . . They set *their eyes* to cast us to the ground . . . (Psalm 17:8, 11).
- "You have tried *my heart,* you have visited me by night, you have tested me, and you will find nothing . . . They close *their hearts* to pity . . . " (Psalm 17:3, 10).
- "*My steps* have held fast to your paths; *my feet* have not slipped . . . *They* have now *surrounded our steps*" (Psalm 17:5, 11).

Consider a third powerful contrast. As our enemies seek to cast us down, God takes up our cause by casting them down. "Deliver my soul from the wicked by your sword, from men by your hand, O LORD" (Psalm 17:13-14). When you believe in true biblical justice, the Lord will confront your enemies. He will bring down their false accusations, and truth will take its proper place.

These dynamic contrasts show the difference between justice that is biblical and that which is pursued of the flesh. David gives us great encouragement for those times when we're surrounded by lies, showing that God's truth arises to deliver us from damaging deceit. Because the Lord faithfully casts down our enemies' lies, we do not have to fear. We are not to stress because we don't have to defend ourselves. All we have to say is, "Lord, I trust in you. You bring me out of every trap and pitfall and set me on a solid rock. I will see you work justice, and my heart will be filled with your glory. You keep me under your protective wings as the apple of your eye." "Hide me in the shadow of your wings" (Psalm 17:8).

David knew that as mortal beings, we can't figure our way out of all the ways Satan comes against us. This includes false accusations. We can't work out ways to justify ourselves against lies that the world hurls at us. If we put our eyes first on God, as we saw Daniel do in the previous chapter, with images of the Ancient of Days wielding righteous judgment from His throne, we will be changed. We'll know that our Redeemer is at work for us.

You may be skeptical. "Are you telling me that if I just trust in God, believing He'll fight my battles, I'll be vindicated in the eyes of the world? Are you saying I don't have to defend myself at all?" The answer, ultimately, is yes. There is a degree to which we participate in the work that God does on our behalf, yet that work begins at His throne. This makes all the difference. When we know we are innocent before the Lord, we can take action from a pure heart. Even though David felt his enemies' accusations—and literal spears and rocks—he showed mercy. When Saul eventually fell in battle, David's allies rejoiced; but David silenced them, saying it was a moment to grieve. When David's son Absalom died in murderous pursuit of his father, David wept in anguish. This reveals a heart after God.

David knew that the Lord judges righteously and that He alone vindicates those who turn to Him. The psalmist Asaph wrote:

> The Mighty One, God the Lord, speaks and summons the earth from the rising of the sun to its setting. Out of Zion, the perfection of beauty, God shines forth. Our God comes; he does not keep silence; before him is a devouring fire, around him a mighty tempest. He calls to the heavens above and to the earth, that he may judge his people: "Gather to me my faithful ones, who made a covenant with me by sacrifice!" The heavens declare his righteousness, for God himself is judge! (Psalm 50:1-6).

In the church, we hear a lot about false voices in the culture around us; but we never hear that God accuses us falsely. If He witnesses against us, it is from His righteous judgment. Yet even if we are guilty, He calls us to gather before Him in the covenant made through Christ's blood to cleanse us of all guilt and condemnation.

A CLEAN HEART

We know that when David declared his innocence, he had already spoken lies, committed adultery, and murdered a man. For insight into David's frame of mind about this, let's turn to Paul. "And to the one who does not work but believes in him who justifies the ungodly, his faith is counted as righteousness" (Rom. 4:5). Paul was making a bold statement here: "We believe in a God Who justifies the ungodly."

To the world's ears, this makes no sense. If we're honest, it makes no sense to our understanding either. To try to comprehend this, let's picture two very different people. First is a criminal who spent forty years robbing and stealing from people and has just begun a lengthy prison sentence. Now think of a missionary who has labored faithfully for forty years, bringing people to Jesus and helping them through their hardships. I want to talk about justification as it applies to these two men.

First, the criminal walks into a prison chapel service and hears a fellow prisoner testifying and preaching of Jesus's righteousness. As the criminal hears this, his heart is stricken; and he falls to his knees, praying, "Jesus, I'm full of shame. Please, rescue me from the life I've lived. I am guilty, and I deserve my sentence. I beg you to save me."

Meanwhile, the missionary leads a worship service in the church that he built for the congregants he led to Christ over decades. Think about how this man must feel as he nears retirement. He can behold the result of his life's work before him, and he feels the opposite of the prisoner's shame. In fact, he feels justified in the fulfilling life he led.

As you consider these two men, how do you feel when you read Paul's words that God "justifies the ungodly" (Rom. 4:5)? Why would God justify the ungodly criminal but perhaps not the missionary who is a picture of godliness? The issue is that God's righteousness and our righteousness are light years from each other. To illustrate, imagine you're taking off in a rocket ship; and out the window, you see the prisoner and the missionary standing on the ground. As the rocket speeds into the atmosphere, the two men disappear below. Eventually, the entire earth disappears. The distance is now immense, unfathomable. That's how far God's righteousness is from ours. What we may consider to be the missionary's righteousness disappears along with everything else. Even his faithful life can't save him; he can only be justified by God's righteousness, birthed in an eternity so infinitely far from the missionary that he must seek the Lord the same way that the prisoner does—on his knees, acknowledging his unworthiness and trusting in God's mercy.

All our best works are as filthy rags before God's righteousness; and all of us are condemned by our sins, even people like the missionary. Paul wrote about this in Philippians 3:

> If anyone else thinks he has reason for confidence in the flesh, I have more: circumcised on the eighth day, of the people of Israel, of the tribe of Benjamin, a Hebrew of Hebrews; as to the law, a Pharisee; as to zeal, a persecutor of the church; as to righteousness under the law, blameless. But whatever gain I had, I counted as loss for the sake of Christ. Indeed, I count everything as loss because of the surpassing worth of knowing Christ Jesus my Lord. For his sake I have suffered the loss of all things and count them as rubbish, in order that I may gain Christ and be found in him, not having a righteousness of my own that comes from the law, but that which comes through faith in Christ, the righteousness from God that depends on faith (Phil. 3:4-9).

Apart from this truth, the missionary has every reason to be confident in his flesh. Yet when we are confronted with the reality of God, as Paul was on the road to Damascus, all of this changes in an instant. Paul saw his righteousness through a completely different lens—the lens of Christ high and lifted up and the blinding brilliance of His righteousness. Suddenly, Paul realized his whole life was not the glorious example of righteousness he had thought it to be; on the contrary, it was a pile of filthy rags. When he wrote that he "counted them as rubbish," he was speaking of his own righteousness.

THE WORST SINNER OF ALL

Once again, we say, "Wait a minute," to Paul's claim. He wrote, "Christ Jesus came into the world to save *sinners, of whom I am the foremost*" (1 Tim. 1:15, my emphasis). Paul was no drunkard, and he wasn't an adulterer. He observed the law; and by that standard, he was, indeed, blameless. So why did he call himself foremost among all sinners? He said it because he saw the sinfulness of his self-righteousness. He said he was the most devout person of his time; yet when it came to righteousness, he was the most damned.

We can't add to our righteousness, even if we are a lifelong missionary. It has absolutely no value. Each of us alike must bow before the holy Lord and say, "I am ungodly, and I need You to make me righteous." So what does this process require? The book of Acts explains, "The times of ignorance God overlooked, but now he commands all people everywhere to repent, because he has fixed a day on which he will judge the world in righteousness by a man whom he has appointed" (Acts 17:30-31). The first act we are commanded to do is repent. Next, note that God has appointed a man to judge us; and of course, that man is Jesus. Justice doesn't come exclusively through judicial courts. The core of all true justice comes through Christ—or "justice by the man," as Martin Luther called it. Jesus is the Man Who undoes our ungodliness and makes us righteous in Him.

"For our sake he made him to be sin who knew no sin, so that in him we might become the righteousness of God" (2 Cor. 5:21). Here is the gospel in one sentence. By the Father's will, Jesus became sin for us so that we, the ungodly, could be justified before the Father. As the passage in Romans tells us, Christ justifies the ungodly by taking our sin upon Himself. When we repent and trust in His finished work on the cross, His righteousness is imputed to us. This sequence of events is what is meant by the theological expression "the exchanged life." In short, Jesus takes our sin upon Himself, nails it to the cross, and buries it in the tomb, never to be raised again. Then He resurrects us to life from the tomb of sin and death and cloaks us in His righteousness. He then transforms our hearts so that our ungodly behaviors begin to fade away.

"It was to show his righteousness at the present time, so that he might be just and the justifier of the one who has faith in Jesus" (Rom. 3:26). Note that in His mercy, Jesus remains just. That means He still condemns sin and brings full wrath because "the wages of sin is death" (Rom. 6:23). Jesus never moves away from being just. The difference is that He places all that wrath upon Himself—all the just punishment and wages—and places on us His resurrection life. He has done for us what we cannot do for ourselves. This truth applies to both the career criminal and the lifelong missionary.

THE RECONCILIATION JESUS HAS CALLED US TO

We're told there can be no reconciliation because there can be no justice; that people of different backgrounds, races, and classes can't come together in any genuine way; that social differences can never be made right. Maybe this is all true apart from Jesus. After all, true justice cannot be found outside of the true Justifier. David knew this, and it is why he never condemned Saul. Nor did he condemn Absalom or Shimei. David needed justice beyond what the world could provide, and he recognized that this came only from the Lord. So David looked prophetically to the Ancient of Days and saw what God could do in his life, and he placed his trust in Him.

David's actions from that point were telling. His life shows us that true justice is having mercy on others, even if they oppose us. That is the beauty and the miracle of the church. People for whom there is no worldly justice find it in God's house where they are accepted, loved, and championed. This includes people whose nations oppose one another; in God's house, they find redemptive love in Christian brotherhood as they pray for peace together, united in Christ.

So let us be careful about what we are willing to accept from "capital-S Social capital-J Justice." Our allegiance and loyalty are to the God of justice, Who justifies the ungodly. Once we experience His mercy, we gratefully work to see His justice heal the world. The world's message of justice is one of hopelessness, despair, anger, and vengeance. God's justice brings mercy, forgiveness, and true reconciliation. None of this is found in our self-righteous ideas of justice or even our greatest works but only in the justifying power of Christ. He makes all who call on Him the apple of his eye, sheltering them safely under His wings.

CHAPTER SEVEN

Psalm 18a
Victory Over Death, the Devil, and the Grave

1 I love you, O Lord, my strength.
2 The Lord is my rock and my fortress and my deliverer,
   my God, my rock, in whom I take refuge,
   my shield, and the horn of my salvation, my stronghold.
3 I call upon the Lord, who is worthy to be praised,
   and I am saved from my enemies.
4 The cords of death encompassed me;
   the torrents of destruction assailed me;
5 the cords of Sheol entangled me;
   the snares of death confronted me.
6 In my distress I called upon the Lord;
   to my God I cried for help.
From his temple he heard my voice,
   and my cry to him reached his ears.
7 Then the earth reeled and rocked;
   the foundations also of the mountains trembled
   and quaked, because he was angry.

8 Smoke went up from his nostrils,
   and devouring fire from his mouth;
   glowing coals flamed forth from him.
9 He bowed the heavens and came down;
   thick darkness was under his feet.
10 He rode on a cherub and flew;
   he came swiftly on the wings of the wind.
11 He made darkness his covering, his canopy around him,
   thick clouds dark with water.
12 Out of the brightness before him
   hailstones and coals of fire broke through his clouds.
13 The Lord also thundered in the heavens,
   and the Most High uttered his voice,
   hailstones and coals of fire.
14 And he sent out his arrows and scattered them;
   he flashed forth lightnings and routed them.
15 Then the channels of the sea were seen,
   and the foundations of the world were laid bare
at your rebuke, O Lord,
   at the blast of the breath of your nostrils.
16 He sent from on high, he took me;
   he drew me out of many waters.
17 He rescued me from my strong enemy
   and from those who hated me,
   for they were too mighty for me.
18 They confronted me in the day of my calamity,
   but the Lord was my support.

19 He brought me out into a broad place;
   he rescued me, because he delighted in me.
20 The Lord dealt with me according to my righteousness;
   according to the cleanness of my hands he rewarded me.
21 For I have kept the ways of the Lord,
   and have not wickedly departed from my God.
22 For all his rules were before me,
   and his statutes I did not put away from me.
23 I was blameless before him,
   and I kept myself from my guilt.
24 So the Lord has rewarded me according to my righteousness,
   according to the cleanness of my hands in his sight.
25 With the merciful you show yourself merciful;
   with the blameless man you show yourself blameless;
26 with the purified you show yourself pure;
   and with the crooked you make yourself seem tortuous.
27 For you save a humble people,
   but the haughty eyes you bring down.
28 For it is you who light my lamp;
   the Lord my God lightens my darkness.
29 For by you I can run against a troop,
   and by my God I can leap over a wall.
30 This God—his way is perfect;
   the word of the Lord proves true;
   he is a shield for all those who take refuge in him.
31 For who is God, but the Lord?
   And who is a rock, except our God?—

32 the God who equipped me with strength
   and made my way blameless.
33 He made my feet like the feet of a deer
   and set me secure on the heights.
34 He trains my hands for war,
   so that my arms can bend a bow of bronze.
35 You have given me the shield of your salvation,
   and your right hand supported me,
   and your gentleness made me great.
36 You gave a wide place for my steps under me,
   and my feet did not slip.
37 I pursued my enemies and overtook them,
   and did not turn back till they were consumed.
38 I thrust them through, so that they were not able to rise;
   they fell under my feet.
39 For you equipped me with strength for the battle;
   you made those who rise against me sink under me.
40 You made my enemies turn their backs to me,
   and those who hated me I destroyed.
41 They cried for help, but there was none to save;
   they cried to the Lord, but he did not answer them.
42 I beat them fine as dust before the wind;
   I cast them out like the mire of the streets.
43 You delivered me from strife with the people;
   you made me the head of the nations;
   people whom I had not known served me.
44 As soon as they heard of me they obeyed me;
   foreigners came cringing to me.

45 Foreigners lost heart
   and came trembling out of their fortresses.
46 The Lord lives, and blessed be my rock,
   and exalted be the God of my salvation—
47 the God who gave me vengeance
   and subdued peoples under me,
48 who rescued me from my enemies;
   yes, you exalted me above those who rose against me;
   you delivered me from the man of violence.
49 For this I will praise you, O Lord, among the nations,
   and sing to your name.
50 Great salvation he brings to his king,
   and shows steadfast love to his anointed,
   to David and his offspring forever.

DAVID'S LENGTHY PSALM 18 PROMISES us victory in life-and-death matters. In fifty verses, he testified of victories no human could achieve on their own: over death, the devil, and the grave. These victories are awe-inspiring gifts, and yet they are central to the faith of every Christian.

By God's grace, I have experienced each of these victories in my life. I resonate with David's witness about them. When he recorded this Psalm, he was remembering all that God had done for him, and what the Lord did was beyond our comprehension. Like David, I often recount God's goodness through the deepest trying matters of my life.

I draw the title for this chapter from verses four and five: "The cords of death encompassed me; the torrents of destruction assailed me; the cords of Sheol entangled me; the snares of death confronted me" (Psalm 18:4-5). The Hebrew word for *encompassed* has the same root as *compass*, summoning the image of a map. David's point here was that everywhere he looked in any direction, death was present. The sight of it was all-encompassing.

His phrase "torrents of destruction assailed me" evokes a powerful river rushing over its banks. The Hebrew word for destruction here is *Belial*, which literally means "Satan" or "the devil." The word for *assailed* suggests firing a deadly weapon, such as an arrow. The phrase *cords of Sheol* summon an image of burial, the grave, being lifeless. When Jesus used the term *Sheol* in the New Testament, He referred to hellfire, the eternal judgment of damnation or separation from God. Likewise, when David spoke of Sheol in Psalm 18, he evoked a nightmarish picture of being bound by cords and dragged into the depths of Hell. His phrase, "the snares of death confronted me," stated, in effect, "I am entangled in the cords of death. I'm being confronted with Hell itself!" Altogether, the picture that David painted in Psalm 18 is one of being surrounded by death, destruction, and evil seeking to snuff out his life.

A MESSAGE OF HOPE AND VICTORY

A few years ago, a doctor discovered a lump on my throat. She performed a biopsy, and I was told that the lump was very common and likely nothing to worry about. I knew something was wrong when the doctor called me on a Thursday night. She informed me that the lump I had was cancerous. I was in shock. My mother had undergone surgeries for cancer many times. Both of my sisters had also dealt with cancer. In fact, my family was assailed by the disease with frightening frequency, encompassing us with endless surgeries and chemotherapies. As I spoke with my doctor about my throat, I was so stunned that I fumbled my words, not knowing what to ask. She explained that the cancer I had was of the thyroid and asked me to come to her office the following Tuesday.

As soon as the shock wore off, I researched thyroid cancer and learned there are two types. For one, there is no cure; once it is diagnosed, you have six months to live. The other thyroid cancer is more easily treated, and the recovery rate is high. For the next five days, I didn't know whether I had six months to live or if I would be treated and healed. Today, as I read Psalm 18, I personally understand what David meant when he said the cords of death encompassed him and that he was confronted with the grave. My diagnosis caused fear and trembling at the thought of dying.

Of course, I prayed for healing; yet I also realized that God ordains our days and that the power of life and death rests fully with Him. The devil may run rampant in certain ways, but he is always under the control of the sovereign Lord. Satan can't do anything outside of God's will. Therefore, the grave is not our last testament; resurrected life is. David addressed this Psalm "to the choirmaster," which tells us, "This is a song the people are going to sing throughout Israel." It signaled a powerful message of hope to come in the verses that followed.

THE SECOND LONGEST INTRODUCTION IN ALL OF THE PSALTERS

David's introduction here holds enough content to stand as a psalm in itself. When he wrote the address calling himself "the servant of the Lord," the same phrase is found in just two other places in all of Scripture. In those other two instances, the only people referred to this way were Moses and Joshua.

David was positioning himself into the same context as these two great prophets of Israel. Moses, of course, brought God's people out of Egypt, through the Red Sea and up to the border of the Promised Land, Canaan. From there, Joshua delivered Israel from all their enemies and led them into Canaan. Both prophets were victorious, with one man leading Israel out of enslavement and the other leading them into a broad place of inheritance. David was saying in Psalm 18, "Like Moses and Joshua, I will testify to God's deliverance of His people out of defeat and into victory." In effect, David was prophesying of Christ, a message more powerful than those of Israel's earlier deliverers.

The book of Hebrews confirms what David was saying. It tells us that far beyond what Moses and Joshua did, only Christ could bring His people into full and complete rest. The Lord anointed Moses and Joshua to perform great and mighty works, miraculous events unmatched in supernatural power. None of those works, however, compared to what Jesus has done. He *is* our Victory over death, the devil, and the grave. David made this comparison to reveal that ultimately, our victory was in the coming Savior.

IMPORTANT CONTEXT FOR DAVID'S TESTIMONY

As we read of David in 2 Samuel 22, he was nearing the end of his life. In this chapter and those that precede it, we see him preparing for death. In chapter twenty-two specifically, David enumerated his deathbed wishes. As he did in Psalm 18, he was looking back on his life and history with the Lord. I picture him composing this psalm as an old man, possibly with gray hair and frail in body. He may have been surrounded by his children, grandchildren, friends, and fellow warriors who fought in Israel's great victorious battles. As David poured out his heart to them, he testified, "God has never failed me or let me down. He never once allowed the enemy to triumph over me. All the cords of death encompassed me, but the Lord gave me victory over them. The torrents of destruction assailed me, but again God gave me victory. Belial, the devil himself, attacked me, but God once more supplied the victory. Death came for me, but look at me today—I'm an old man who has lived a full life to a ripe age. I have seen the victory of the Lord in every area of my life. I have known hardships and struggles, and I have faced death; but the Lord delivered me out of them all."

Again, I relate with David. I have four children and nine grandchildren with hopefully more on the way. I can picture a day in the future when I reflect on my loved ones as David did, knowing my time is short. I'll be able to tell them, "Cancer attacked my thyroid, but the Lord blessed me with healing. I was in a car wreck that broke my back in two places and wasn't sure I would ever walk again. Look at me now, standing, walking, and running. I've battled depression, and God gave me victory over it. As a young man, I battled insecurity, as well as an addiction to pornography; but God set me free from it all. I've been through trials with coworkers who falsely accused me and spoke evil of me, but God saw me through. In all these things, the Lord brought me into a broad place with a song of victory."

I draw every bit of this from David's introduction to Psalm 18. Even if we never get to verse one of this Psalm, we already have a complete sermon from the phrase, "the day when the Lord delivered (David) from the hand of all his enemies." I urge you to circle that word *all*. Circle it not just in your Bible but also in your mind, and let nothing assail it. At various times in your life, you will be overwhelmed by thoughts like, "I won't make it. I'm in death's grip, and I'm going to be defeated." When these thoughts come, look at the word you circled—*all*—and remind yourself that no pressing situation ever has power over you. God's hand is over your life at all times, with sovereign control over every trial. Not a single enemy has prevailed over you, nor will it ever.

DAVID'S MOST POWERFUL STRUGGLES

David's greatest struggle might have been with his pride over great prowess in warfare. Perhaps his struggle was with fear or doubt. Maybe it had to do with the lust that led to his adultery with Bathsheba and his murderous scheme which killed her husband. Each of us sees the external battles God has won for us; but sometimes, our greatest worry is over our internal struggles. We wonder, "Will I ever overcome this anxiety? When will I break free of this addiction? Will my broken spirit ever be healed? Will I ever find a cure for this physical affliction?" Deep inside, the constant refrain for many is, "Will I ever? Will I ever? Will I ever?"

Through all his battles, David was able to look back on his life and say, "God freed me. He forgave me, delivered me, and accepted me. He caused me to be righteous and holy. He gave me clean hands and a pure heart. He did it all for me!" God can do all of this for your heart and mine. Indeed, He has never stopped doing it for us, and He never will. His people will see His deliverance in everything.

In David's introduction to this Psalm, he said that once he was delivered from his enemies, he sang a song of victory. This is very significant because as the first seventeen psalms show, David's constant cry was, "How long, O Lord? When will I be delivered? When will my enemies stop assaulting me? When will you break through and give me victory?"

It is easy to understand where David's cries came from. His life was a constant series of ups and downs, mountains and valleys, failures and successes, victories and defeats. Here in Psalm 18, however, he was stating, "My cry is no longer, 'How long?' The battle is now over. Victory has been won!"

We don't have to wait until old age to see God's history in our lives. All of us face certain battles; and many of us are asking, "How long do I have to wait, Lord?" God answers that question with Psalm 18. Because of David's testimony, we, too, can say, "One day, ten years ago, God delivered me when my I lost my job, leading me into new work. One day, six years ago, He delivered me from heart failure and into fully recovered health. Ten months ago, He restored my child to me after years of alienation."

On and on, our lives are filled with testimonies of His work. He has never allowed the enemy to prevail over us. Maybe you once felt that God's Word was dead to you, but the Lord brought it alive in your heart again. Maybe when you thought sin would overwhelm you, He sent His Spirit to show you a way of escape. As you recount any such deliverances, you are able to sing a song of victory. So sing it loudly, as David did, with harps and lyres or with ear buds. You've been given a victory song!

WAITING TO SEE YOUR DELIVERANCE

David's message was that even though we may have to wait for it, the day of our deliverance is surely coming. I want to both challenge and encourage you with a message my father once preached. It's not from Psalm 18, but it applies to one of this psalm's themes. The message was a sermon titled "Right Song, Wrong Side." It was based on the song of Moses after God delivered Israel from the Egyptian army at the Red Sea.

God's people were trapped at the shore, fearing for their lives as the Egyptians fast approached. Just in time, God miraculously parted the waves so they could cross safely through to the other side. As the Egyptians tried to pursue, God brought the waves crashing down on them, destroying Pharaoh's army. It was a miraculous victory, and the Israelites broke into song, "The Lord has rescued us from the hands of our enemies!"

A song naturally comes to our lips when we see victories. In Psalm 18, however, David wanted us to know that God is so faithful we can trust Him for victory *before* we see it unfolding. My father's sermon on this subject was like David's message. Even when we can't envision our deliverance, we nevertheless have a victory song to sing. The Lord won't ever allow death, the devil, or the grave to prevail over us. So if we can learn to praise Him for victory on the right side, before we see deliverance, we'll have Heaven's joy and peace when we need it most. We can walk through our storms knowing that no weapon can be used against us because our Redeemer lives.

AN OUTLINE DIVIDING PSALM 18

In the first nineteen verses of this psalm, David spoke of three front lines of spiritual battle. He informed us that in all three of these arenas—on earth, in Heaven, and below earth—we can possess a song of victory. The first line of battle, described in verses one through eight, takes place on the earth. This battlefront is one of literal life and death. It is why throughout, the psalter David used the phrase, "the land of the living." He was saying, in essence, "I know a time is coming when I'll pass away from this earth, yet I know the Lord will resurrect me."

Of course, this truth is expressed more directly in the New Testament, with the added joy that we'll spend eternity with Jesus. In His presence, there won't be any more tears, sorrow, heartache, or sin. However, according to David, we inhabit the land of the living on earth as fragile humans. Our life in this world is one of groaning and waging battles of life and death.

The second battle line, described in verses nine through fourteen, involves the heavens. This is a cosmic, spiritual battle between light and darkness. In the first battle, which takes place on earth, we wonder, "Are we going to win or lose? Will we lose our lives or be spared?" In the battle of the heavens, the conflict takes place in an unseen realm; and our role is one of prayer. We can have an effect on this battle, but it is somewhat beyond us.

The third and final battle line, found in verses fifteen through nineteen, involves a battle "under" the earth, perhaps meaning the seas. This is a battle between drowning and rescue, between being overwhelmed by enemies with no air in our lungs or being pulled up and saved. Studying each of these battlefronts will help us profoundly in our daily walk of faith.

THE EARTH REELING AND ROCKING.

The first spiritual battlefront, which takes place on the earth, impacts daily lives. In David's life, this battle took place when he was threatened and fled, hiding among rocks and caves. Saul had placed a bounty on his head, and David and his men were on guard for their lives around the clock. At times, they might have despaired. As David wrote in the last part of verse seventeen, "They were too mighty for me" (Psalm 18:17).

David could defeat giants, bears, and lions; he could bring down armies of thousands, with people singing songs about his exploits. However, there was something about this season of life that affected him deeply. "They confronted me in the day of my calamity" (Psalm 18:18). He admitted, "This one threw me off. It hit me in a different way, confounding me. I was overwhelmed."

At this point in Psalm 18, I want to circle back to the opening verse to show something very revealing. David began the psalm by saying very simply, "I love you, O Lord, my strength" (Psalm 18:1). Friend, this is an example of singing the right song on the *right* side.

You see, David had always loved the Lord; yet as he prepared to recount his history with God, he was filled with a special kind of love. He was saying, in effect, "Lord, as I consider all that You have done for me, I am incredibly blessed. You healed me. You delivered me. You saved me and rescued my family. You are my Savior and Lord, and I love You." He had decided, in essence, "If I'm going to sing a song of deliverance, the first words out of my mouth are going to be, 'I love you, Lord.'" May these also be the first words out of our mouths.

David continued, "The Lord is my rock and my fortress and my deliverer, my God, my rock, in whom I take refuge, my shield, and the horn of my salvation, my stronghold" (Psalm 18:2). What an incredible list of protective powers. David was telling us that God had replaced them all. The Lord had become each of these things to him. David's salvation was no longer found in such powerful protections but in the Lord Himself.

Today, we, too, rely on a long list of things to get us through life: a home, a car, money in the bank, doctors, and specialists. The Lord supersedes all these things. Our lives are set in a broad place of victory that is supplied by the Lord's power alone.

WHEN GOD HEARS YOUR CRY

David testified that when he was distressed by terrors, "In my distress I called upon the Lord; to my God I cried for help. From his temple he heard my voice, and my cry to him reached his ears" (Psalm 18:6). The first thing to say about this verse is that your cry matters to the Lord. He loves when our cry reaches His ears; it stirs Him to rise up powerfully on our behalf. It also changes things. Note how God reacted when David's cry reached Him: "Then the earth reeled and rocked; the foundations also of the mountains trembled and quaked, because he was angry. Smoke went up from his nostrils, and devouring fire from his mouth; glowing coals flamed forth from him" (Psalm 18:7-8).

You may never have had an advocate in your life; but when you cry out to the Lord, He rises up for you in an incredible way. He does this immediately upon hearing your cry. It happens then, as David wrote—not later, not before, but right away. At the moment of your cry, something begins to change in your circumstance, though it may not be apparent. As David stated, when God does come, it is not with trivialities but with fury. For these reasons, it is important not to lose hope but to pray without ceasing. He hears your cry and acts.

THE SECOND BATTLELINE IN THE HEAVENS

When God hears our prayers, He not only enters the land of the living to be with us; He also immediately engages the enemy for us. David described this by saying, "He bowed the heavens and came down; thick darkness was under his feet" (Psalm 18:9). We know that God exists in unapproachable light; there is no darkness in Him at all. So, according to David's description, God descends to our need with powerful light, entering the darkness that encompasses us. This happens as quickly as David could possibly imagine. "He rode on a cherub and flew; he came swiftly on the wings of the wind" (Psalm 18:10).

Simply put, God was there in the midst of David's problem in an instant. As the Lord descended, more of His awesome light diminished the darkness in His path. In practical terms, God was reversing the powers of worldliness surrounding David. He made darkness submit to Him.

"Out of the brightness before him hailstones and coals of fire broke through his clouds" (Psalm 18:12). David's visual language here helps us envision the powerful way God's glory enters our corners of shame and our places of defeat. These hailstones and fiery coals comprise a picture of God's will being done "'on earth as it is in heaven'" (Matt. 6:10).

Verse twenty-eight serves as a kind of capstone to it all. "For it is you who light my lamp; the Lord my God lightens my darkness" (Psalm 18:28). Everywhere God places His foot, darkness flees; and light replaces it. This is "the goodness of [God]" manifesting "in the land of the living" (Psalm 27:13).

The prophet Isaiah spoke of this great truth, and praise songs have been built upon it. "Arise, shine, for your light has come, and the glory of the Lord has risen upon you. For behold, darkness shall cover the earth, and thick darkness the peoples; but the Lord will arise upon you, and his glory will be seen upon you" (Isa. 60:1-2). The darkness in our world today is unmistakable, equaling—or, perhaps, surpassing—that of Sodom and Gomorrah. Like David, though, we can cry out knowing God's promise to hear us and begin our deliverance immediately. As this happens, the world will see the difference in darkness and light and be drawn to the Lord, Who delivers His people. "And nations shall come to your light, and kings to the brightness of your rising" (Isa. 60:3).

God has a plan. He does not just stand by and say, "I can't do anything about this." He enters into the darkness of our affliction, trouble, pain, and brokenness. At that point, according to David, "He sent out his arrows and scattered them; he flashed forth lightnings and routed them" (Psalm 18:14). This victorious image was a prophecy of the coming Christ, Who chases away all darkness from our circumstances and in our hearts.

THE THIRD BATTLELINE: BATTLE OF THE SEAS

The battle of the seas is where we are overwhelmed by things from below earth, meaning the pits of Hell. Primarily, I think of the flood of filth in our culture, a gross darkness that emerges from Hell to cover the land. At times, this flood is almost enough to drown us. Be assured, God steps into this battle, too.

> Then the channels of the sea were seen, and the foundations of the world were laid bare at your rebuke, O Lord, at the blast of the breath of your nostrils. He sent from on high, he took me; he drew me out of many waters. He rescued me from my strong enemy and from those who hated me, for they were too mighty for me. They confronted me in the day of my calamity, but the Lord was my support. He brought me out into a broad place; he rescued me, because he delighted in me (Psalm 18:15-19).

The Hebrew word for "channels" in the opening phrase here can mean a stream or river, but it can also mean something stout or strong. The picture that David painted here was one of a stout, unyielding darkness covering the earth. Then a cry went up; and Jesus descended from above, turning darkness into light. That light exposed the forces of Hell surfacing to attack us. David testified that God blows away these channels of darkness; but even so, a battle remains below. Satan does not give up, despite seeing that every hellish thing will pass away in the light of God's glory.

DESTRUCTION OF THE POWER OF DEATH

Death's power was destroyed on the cross. Christ didn't just change our circumstances with His crucifixion, burial, and resurrection. He won the final battle by conquering death and the fear of it. In doing so, He has given us victory, no matter what happens in life. We no longer have to fear because He has conquered in the most difficult place of all.

"He sent from on high, he took me; he drew me out of many waters" (Psalm 18:16). Some of us have a deathly problem standing in front of us. Others of us face many deathly problems. If we're being harangued and harassed on every side and feel like we're drowning, we don't have to fear. God draws us out of every threatening river.

I want to return now to the promise of the introduction: "The Lord delivered him from the hand of all his enemies" (Psalm 18). Not only is there a cosmic victory in the heavens; but God also comes down to rescue us, picking us up and removing us from the hands of strong enemies. He hears our cry and defeats our enemies, giving us victory over each one.

God's delivering power does not stop there. David wrote, "He brought me out *into* a broad place" (Psalm 18:19, my emphasis). The Lord not only brought David *out* of a threatening situation; He also brought Him *into* a place of blessing. This brings to mind Moses and Joshua. God led Israel not only *out* of Egypt but *into* Canaan, the Promised Land. In Hebrew, the word for *broad* means an increase, an enlargement, a bigger inheritance than imagined. If the enemy has you pressed down and bound, Jesus has freed you to walk widely through green pastures. The place He brings you into is broader than any you've experienced before.

Finally, David summed up this beginning section of Psalm 18 with, "He rescued me, because he delighted in me" (Psalm 18:19). He was saying, "Lord, You not only delivered me from death, the devil, and the grave; but you also delighted to bring me into a broad place. I now have a greater song to sing, a greater knowledge of You, and a greater ability to shout with joy, 'I love You, O Lord.'" Because of Jesus, we can say as David did, "Lord, I have nothing to fear. You deliver me from all my enemies, giving me hope, peace, and joy. You have planted in me supernatural stability; and Your work in my life is seen by my children, grandchildren, siblings, fellow Christians, and coworkers. They can see that when the most threatening torrents come, all is well with my soul. I love You, O Lord."

CHAPTER EIGHT

Psalm 18b
The Lord Is My Rock and My Fortress

1 I love you, O Lord, my strength.
2 The Lord is my rock and my fortress and my deliverer,
  my God, my rock, in whom I take refuge,
  my shield, and the horn of my salvation, my stronghold.
3 I call upon the Lord, who is worthy to be praised,
  and I am saved from my enemies.
4 The cords of death encompassed me;
  the torrents of destruction assailed me;
5 the cords of Sheol entangled me;
  the snares of death confronted me.
6 In my distress I called upon the Lord;
  to my God I cried for help.
From his temple he heard my voice,
  and my cry to him reached his ears.
7 Then the earth reeled and rocked;
  the foundations also of the mountains trembled
  and quaked, because he was angry.

8 Smoke went up from his nostrils,
   and devouring fire from his mouth;
   glowing coals flamed forth from him.
9 He bowed the heavens and came down;
   thick darkness was under his feet.
10 He rode on a cherub and flew;
   he came swiftly on the wings of the wind.
11 He made darkness his covering, his canopy around him,
   thick clouds dark with water.
12 Out of the brightness before him
   hailstones and coals of fire broke through his clouds.
13 The Lord also thundered in the heavens,
   and the Most High uttered his voice,
   hailstones and coals of fire.
14 And he sent out his arrows and scattered them;
   he flashed forth lightnings and routed them.
15 Then the channels of the sea were seen,
   and the foundations of the world were laid bare
at your rebuke, O Lord,
   at the blast of the breath of your nostrils.
16 He sent from on high, he took me;
   he drew me out of many waters.
17 He rescued me from my strong enemy
   and from those who hated me,
   for they were too mighty for me.
18 They confronted me in the day of my calamity,
   but the Lord was my support.

19 He brought me out into a broad place;
   he rescued me, because he delighted in me.
20 The Lord dealt with me according to my righteousness;
   according to the cleanness of my hands he rewarded me.
21 For I have kept the ways of the Lord,
   and have not wickedly departed from my God.
22 For all his rules were before me,
   and his statutes I did not put away from me.
23 I was blameless before him,
   and I kept myself from my guilt.
24 So the Lord has rewarded me according to my righteousness,
   according to the cleanness of my hands in his sight.
25 With the merciful you show yourself merciful;
   with the blameless man you show yourself blameless;
26 with the purified you show yourself pure;
   and with the crooked you make yourself seem tortuous.
27 For you save a humble people,
   but the haughty eyes you bring down.
28 For it is you who light my lamp;
   the Lord my God lightens my darkness.
29 For by you I can run against a troop,
   and by my God I can leap over a wall.
30 This God—his way is perfect;
   the word of the Lord proves true;
   he is a shield for all those who take refuge in him.
31 For who is God, but the Lord?
   And who is a rock, except our God?—

32 the God who equipped me with strength
  and made my way blameless.
33 He made my feet like the feet of a deer
  and set me secure on the heights.
34 He trains my hands for war,
  so that my arms can bend a bow of bronze.
35 You have given me the shield of your salvation,
  and your right hand supported me,
  and your gentleness made me great.
36 You gave a wide place for my steps under me,
  and my feet did not slip.
37 I pursued my enemies and overtook them,
  and did not turn back till they were consumed.
38 I thrust them through, so that they were not able to rise;
  they fell under my feet.
39 For you equipped me with strength for the battle;
  you made those who rise against me sink under me.
40 You made my enemies turn their backs to me,
  and those who hated me I destroyed.
41 They cried for help, but there was none to save;
  they cried to the Lord, but he did not answer them.
42 I beat them fine as dust before the wind;
  I cast them out like the mire of the streets.
43 You delivered me from strife with the people;
  you made me the head of the nations;
  people whom I had not known served me.

44 As soon as they heard of me they obeyed me;
   foreigners came cringing to me.
45 Foreigners lost heart
   and came trembling out of their fortresses.
46 The Lord lives, and blessed be my rock,
   and exalted be the God of my salvation—
47 the God who gave me vengeance
   and subdued peoples under me,
48 who rescued me from my enemies;
   yes, you exalted me above those who rose against me;
   you delivered me from the man of violence.
49 For this I will praise you, O Lord, among the nations,
   and sing to your name.
50 Great salvation he brings to his king,
   and shows steadfast love to his anointed,
   to David and his offspring forever.

WE'RE STILL IN PSALM 18, and we will be for another chapter, all of which is needed to accommodate this packed and lengthy song by David. In the preceding chapter, he wrote of having victory over death, the devil, and the grave. He concluded that opening section by saying, "He brought me out into a broad place; he rescued me, because he delighted in me" (Psalm 18:19).

At times, I've thought this verse came across as a little strange. David seemed to be saying, "God did all these things—hearing my cry and giving me victory—because I am His delight." This can sound as if David is overemphasizing his place in God's heart. Then, in the next section of the psalm (which we'll examine in this chapter), David continued to speak in similar terms.

> The Lord dealt with me according to my righteousness; according to the cleanness of my hands he rewarded me. For I have kept the ways of the Lord, and have not wickedly departed from my God. For all his rules were before me, and his statutes I did not put away from me. I was blameless before him, and I kept myself from my guilt. So the Lord has rewarded me according to my righteousness, according to the cleanness of my hands in his sight. With the merciful you show yourself merciful; with the blameless man you show yourself blameless; with the purified you show yourself pure; and with the crooked you make yourself seem tortuous. For you save a humble people, but the haughty eyes you bring down. For it is you who light my lamp; the Lord my God lightens my darkness (Psalm 18:20-28).

David's language here may sound self-congratulatory, but the context indicates otherwise. After all, he stated in his introduction to Psalm 18 that his reason for writing it was that God delivered him from all his enemies. With that said, I believe there are three major points David wanted to make in this section. The first is that righteousness is a result of covenant. The second is that righteousness reaps rewards. The third is that righteousness reaps results. Examining these not only will help us understand David's message in this section but will also help us in our walk with Jesus.

RIGHTEOUSNESS AS A RESULT OF THE COVENANT

I think C.H. Spurgeon said it best that God first gives holiness and then rewards it. In other words, holiness comes to us from God alone;

and then we find rewards as we walk holy before Him. This sheds light on David's claim that "the Lord has rewarded me according to my righteousness, according to the cleanness of my hands in his sight" (Psalm 18:24). David's statement here could easily be misread as claiming a self-righteousness, as in, "I earned God's reward because He's on my side. All the favor of God in my life is because I'm a good person, keeping His rules and statutes. He looks down from Heaven and says, 'There goes a servant who is holy, just and pure in himself.'"

No, David understood that his righteousness was not of his own making, that as Paul wrote, "None is righteous, no, not one" (Rom. 3:10). David clarified this in verse twenty-seven: "For you save a humble people, but the haughty eyes you bring down" (Psalm 18:27). The word *save* here can mean, "You, Lord, make us righteous, blameless and clean. You bring us out of darkness and into light, making us worthy of your delight." David said this because he fully understood his own sinfulness.

The righteousness that David spoke of was like Abraham's, a righteousness by faith. When he said of God, "You save a humble person," he might as well have been testifying, "I once was lost but now am found. You, Lord, have made me spotless and clean and have given me a pure heart."

So David isn't to be judged for his appearance of self-righteousness. On the contrary, I hope we all can learn from his example. We live in a generation when people are told only how good they are, that nothing they do is wrong, that they're worthy and deserving of all things. David's stance in this psalm was just the opposite. He understood very well just how darkened his heart was by sin. That's why he humbled himself to be saved. He declared in another psalm, "The sacrifices of God are a broken spirit; a broken and contrite heart, O God, you will not despise" (Psalm 51:17). The contrite are the ones God will cleanse and make righteous.

THE STAIN OF SIN

David taught, "Behold, I was brought forth in iniquity, and in sin did my mother conceive me" (Psalm 51:5). David knew he wasn't born holy, clean, or righteous. Something had to happen from outside himself to bring about any change in his heart. This truth was demonstrated after David committed the most grievous sins of his life. The prophet Nathan confronted him about his adultery and murder, and it broke David. He knew he couldn't change his sinful state by changing his behavior. He had to have a change of heart. That process began when he humbled himself in contrition, repenting before the Lord.

David's posture was in total contrast to that of Saul, when the latter was confronted with his sin. In truth, Saul's sin seemed a lot lesser than David's. The Lord had instructed Saul to destroy every living thing from the enemy army that Israel conquered; but instead of obeying, Saul spared some of the people and spoils.

When the prophet Samuel arrived and confronted him, Saul confessed his sin; but his attitude was different from David's. He admitted fearing the fleshly judgment of the people rather than the holy judgment of God. That kind of confession wasn't true repentance but rather an excuse. What Saul said next was even more revealing: "Now therefore, please pardon my sin and return with me that I may bow before the Lord" (1 Sam. 15:25). Saul sought God vicariously through Samuel, rather than from his own heart.

A lot of Christians today live the way Saul did. Instead of having their own relationship with Jesus, they rely on answers from books and sermons. True repentance is dependent on a relationship with the Lord, as David's example showed. If we don't have genuine intimacy with God, we can't expect to have genuine righteousness but only a manmade form of it. That kind of righteousness has a performance aspect instead of a genuine change of heart.

Saul couldn't say as David did, "My hands have been made clean and my heart made pure by the Lord." He had no victory song because he didn't face up to being born into iniquity. Like David, Isaiah, and Peter, all of us are right to fall before the Lord crying, "My heart is undone because I'm unclean." Such broken cries burst from a knowledge of fallenness and the need to be saved.

BORN OUT OF THE NEW COVENANT OF CHRIST

The righteousness that David referred to begins with repentance, and it comes to us through Jesus' work on the cross. Any cleansing from sin that we experience doesn't come through endless sacrifices we make over and over again. Hebrews tells us Jesus' sacrifice for us was once and for all. When David said, "For it is you who light my lamp; the Lord my God lightens my darkness" (Psalm 18:28), I envision God's light washing us clean of our darkness. His presence rescues us from our lost state, making us blameless and giving us clean hands and a pure heart. In essence, David was saying, "Lord, the light of your grace drew me out of my dark pit. You transformed me from what I once was."

We recognize this transformation as the result of the New Covenant. Through it, God has said, "I have put in you a new heart. I will empower you to walk in obedience to My commands." In short, our movement toward God is always grace-driven. Any righteousness we have arrives as a gift from above, coming to us through genuine repentance and knowing who we are in Christ. David affirmed this when he wrote, "With the purified you show yourself pure" (Psalm 18:26). The word *purified* is passive, meaning we've been acted upon by an outside source (the blood of Jesus and the power of the Holy Spirit). We didn't purify ourselves; our purification came by way of the New Covenant.

In addition, this verse says God shows Himself pure to us, meaning He reveals to us His awesome purity. The next part of this verse tells us that the opposite happens with those of a crooked spirit, people who don't understand their fallen nature or the gravity of their sin: "and with the crooked you make yourself seem tortuous" (Psalm 18:26). It feels like torture to try being righteous on your own, simply because it's impossible to accomplish. If you've ever tried to pull yourself out of sin by sheer will, to make yourself clean and holy by self-effort, you know how unbearable the effort is. It's so torturous that you eventually give up. Without the power of the New Covenant enabling you, the straight paths of righteousness are impossible.

If your righteousness is born of the New Covenant, however, you reap precious promises and rewards. "The Lord dealt with me according to my righteousness; according to the cleanness of my hands he rewarded me" (Psalm 18:20). David was saying, "Lord, because you've cleansed me and made me righteous, you now deal with me in a certain way. It would be totally different if I were impure and rebellious."

This is one way righteousness has rewards. When David said that all his enemies had been defeated, that, too, is a reward of the righteous. Another reward, as the verse above shows, is having clean hands after they've been filthy. The Holy Spirit not only makes us clean but keeps us clean. In these ways and more, the righteousness we're given leads to great rewards.

RIGHTEOUSNESS REAPS RESULTS

Righteousness empowers us to live a holy life, plain and simple. God's purpose in making us righteous isn't so that we become couch potatoes, selfishly concerned with our own interests. God's impartation of His righteousness moves us to think, feel, move, and walk out the life-giving servanthood of the gospel. You see, one result of righteousness is that our behavior changes—our language, convictions, interactions, and decision-making. If none of these things have changed in you, you probably ought to reexamine whether you're walking in true repentance. Understanding the gravity of your sin will move you to seek the Spirit's work in your life, a work you can't do for yourself. By His New Covenant, the Lord puts in you a new heart, one that's inclined toward transformation. Thus, as you fail (and you will), you'll desire never to sin in the same way again.

"For I have kept the ways of the Lord, and have not wickedly departed from my God" (Psalm 18:21). This verse contains two phrases crucial to our walk with the Lord. The first is the phrase "I have," and the second is "I have not." The first phrase focuses on the positive ways we are graced and empowered to new behavior. With a new heart and a new mind, we understand God's ways and desire to keep them.

Equally important is the second part of this verse, to rid ourselves of the things that separate us from God. New Covenant grace empowers us to say, "I have not departed from the Lord or dismissed His ways. I no longer indulge in the things that once dragged me down. I love my old friends, witness to them, and pray for their salvation; but I do not give myself over to the spirit of this world."

Paul made this same distinction about the Christians in Corinth. "Do not be deceived: neither the sexually immoral, nor idolaters, nor adulterers, nor men who practice homosexuality, nor thieves, nor the greedy, nor drunkards, nor revilers, nor swindlers will inherit the kingdom of God. And such were some of you. But you were washed, you were sanctified, you were justified in the name of the Lord Jesus Christ and by the Spirit of our God" (1 Cor. 6:9-11).

So how do we keep the Lord's ways and forsake the ways of the world? David answered, "For all his rules were before me, and his statutes I did not put away from me" (Psalm 18:22). We stay in God's Word. We keep in His fellowship. We meditate on what we read and hear preached and see in the lives of our fellow believers. In short, we keep the light of God's lamp continually before us to illuminate our path. "For it is you who light my lamp; the Lord my God lightens my darkness" (Psalm 18:28).

PICK AND CHOOSE

Few of us have trouble obeying the command to pray for others. But obeying the command to forgive others isn't so easy. David was no different from us, yet he could say, "His statutes I did not put away from me" (Psalm 18:22). If we have a New Covenant heart, we won't want to be forced to forgive. Instead, we'll want to overcome our resistance to forgive.

At this point, I go back to David's words, "For you save a humble people, but the haughty eyes you bring down" (Psalm 18:27). There is never a time that our righteous standing before God will move us to be haughty, convinced we know it all. That doesn't happen with grace-driven righteousness. It would blunt the very humility that drives us to God. Our utter dependency on the Lord actually empowers us, so that we can say, "I thank God none of this depends on me. I don't have to try to be righteous in my own strength. It's not I but *He* Who delivers me from all my enemies." That is joy to live by.

CHAPTER NINE

Psalm 18c
Mo(u)rning Has Broken

1 I love you, O Lord, my strength.
2 The Lord is my rock and my fortress and my deliverer,
   my God, my rock, in whom I take refuge,
   my shield, and the horn of my salvation, my stronghold.
3 I call upon the Lord, who is worthy to be praised,
   and I am saved from my enemies.
4 The cords of death encompassed me;
   the torrents of destruction assailed me;
5 the cords of Sheol entangled me;
   the snares of death confronted me.
6 In my distress I called upon the Lord;
   to my God I cried for help.
From his temple he heard my voice,
   and my cry to him reached his ears.
7 Then the earth reeled and rocked;
   the foundations also of the mountains trembled
   and quaked, because he was angry.

8 Smoke went up from his nostrils,
   and devouring fire from his mouth;
   glowing coals flamed forth from him.
9 He bowed the heavens and came down;
   thick darkness was under his feet.
10 He rode on a cherub and flew;
   he came swiftly on the wings of the wind.
11 He made darkness his covering, his canopy around him,
   thick clouds dark with water.
12 Out of the brightness before him
   hailstones and coals of fire broke through his clouds.
13 The Lord also thundered in the heavens,
   and the Most High uttered his voice,
   hailstones and coals of fire.
14 And he sent out his arrows and scattered them;
   he flashed forth lightnings and routed them.
15 Then the channels of the sea were seen,
   and the foundations of the world were laid bare
at your rebuke, O Lord,
   at the blast of the breath of your nostrils.
16 He sent from on high, he took me;
   he drew me out of many waters.
17 He rescued me from my strong enemy
   and from those who hated me,
   for they were too mighty for me.
18 They confronted me in the day of my calamity,
   but the Lord was my support.

19 He brought me out into a broad place;
   he rescued me, because he delighted in me.
20 The Lord dealt with me according to my righteousness;
   according to the cleanness of my hands he rewarded me.
21 For I have kept the ways of the Lord,
   and have not wickedly departed from my God.
22 For all his rules were before me,
   and his statutes I did not put away from me.
23 I was blameless before him,
   and I kept myself from my guilt.
24 So the Lord has rewarded me according to my righteousness,
   according to the cleanness of my hands in his sight.
25 With the merciful you show yourself merciful;
   with the blameless man you show yourself blameless;
26 with the purified you show yourself pure;
   and with the crooked you make yourself seem tortuous.
27 For you save a humble people,
   but the haughty eyes you bring down.
28 For it is you who light my lamp;
   the Lord my God lightens my darkness.
29 For by you I can run against a troop,
   and by my God I can leap over a wall.
30 This God—his way is perfect;
   the word of the Lord proves true;
   he is a shield for all those who take refuge in him.
31 For who is God, but the Lord?
   And who is a rock, except our God?—

32 the God who equipped me with strength
   and made my way blameless.
33 He made my feet like the feet of a deer
   and set me secure on the heights.
34 He trains my hands for war,
   so that my arms can bend a bow of bronze.
35 You have given me the shield of your salvation,
   and your right hand supported me,
   and your gentleness made me great.
36 You gave a wide place for my steps under me,
   and my feet did not slip.
37 I pursued my enemies and overtook them,
   and did not turn back till they were consumed.
38 I thrust them through, so that they were not able to rise;
   they fell under my feet.
39 For you equipped me with strength for the battle;
   you made those who rise against me sink under me.
40 You made my enemies turn their backs to me,
   and those who hated me I destroyed.
41 They cried for help, but there was none to save;
   they cried to the Lord, but he did not answer them.
42 I beat them fine as dust before the wind;
   I cast them out like the mire of the streets.
43 You delivered me from strife with the people;
   you made me the head of the nations;
   people whom I had not known served me.
44 As soon as they heard of me they obeyed me;
   foreigners came cringing to me.

45 Foreigners lost heart
and came trembling out of their fortresses.
46 The Lord lives, and blessed be my rock,
and exalted be the God of my salvation—
47 the God who gave me vengeance
and subdued peoples under me,
48 who rescued me from my enemies;
yes, you exalted me above those who rose against me;
you delivered me from the man of violence.
49 For this I will praise you, O Lord, among the nations,
and sing to your name.
50 Great salvation he brings to his king,
and shows steadfast love to his anointed,
to David and his offspring forever.

THERE ARE TWO WAYS TO read the title I've given this chapter. First, there is morning as in daybreak, with the sun breaking through darkness. Second, there is the dissipation of sorrow, as in mourning. Either way, this chapter is one of joy and victory over our enemies.

We began Psalm 18 by seeing that God gives us victory over death, the devil, and the grave. Here in the final section, verses twenty-eight through fifty, we see how God trains our hands for battle. We also see His hand move in a mighty way to crush every work that the enemy brings against us.

Two chapters ago, in verses four and five, David laid out the core crisis for every Christian as the cords of death bound him in terror. Ultimately, though, God was using David's trials to train him to do battle against fear, specifically the fear of death. This particular fear causes anyone to live in anxiety, stress, and tribulation of soul. For David, the enemy in this battle wasn't only death but also Belial, or Satan, who raged against him. Finally, there was Sheol, or the grave, including Hell and judgment. The thought of this filled David with a fear of not being worthy; he was overwhelmed by the thought of his sins and feared he deserved judgment.

As David reflected on each of these fears, he saw that he was being trained by the Lord to overcome each one. These are the same enemies you and I face in life. According to the prophet Isaiah, "Behold, darkness shall cover the earth, and thick darkness the peoples" (Isa. 60:2). We are surrounded by gross darkness, with hellish forces spewing venom against us, our family, and our faith community. In this final section of Psalm 18, we learn how God's light actually fights off darkness and what our role is in the battle.

THREE TYPES OF EQUIPPING

We need to be equipped for battle, for victory, and for the morning to be broken. In three passages within this section, David showed us how we find all this equipping:

- We find equipment for victory by the knowledge of God (vv. 30-31).
- We find equipment for battle by having the Lord train our hands for war (vv. 29-41).
- We find our equipment for morning to be broken by being exalted by God (vv. 42-50). This last part may sound strange to say, but it is very much a part of the victory God brings to our life.

Let's look at how we are equipped through the knowledge of God. Throughout the Bible, light represents the knowledge of the Lord. When we're confronted by the powers of Hell, God raises up his glorious light; and we have a breakthrough. "The LORD my God lightens my darkness. For by you I can run against a troop, and by my God I can leap over a wall" (Psalm 18:28-29).

Knowledge of the Lord brings power that helps to create victory. "The people who know their God shall stand firm and take action" (Dan. 11:32). The converse might be true as well. People who don't have knowledge of God struggle to find strength for victory. David will show us how only a knowledge of the Lord can equip us for battle and help us triumph over the powers of darkness.

"For who is God, but the LORD?" (Psalm 18:31). This question addresses a theological question, and the answer is in the phrase that follows. "And who is a rock, except our God?—the God who equipped me with strength" (Psalm 18:31-32). Here is a foundational truth about the Lord that answers a core question at the bottom of our hearts: "What is God like?" David answered, "Here is what he's like: He is all-powerful, omnipotent, a Rock."

David then built on this knowledge. "This God—his way is perfect; the word of the Lord proves true; he is a shield for all those who take refuge in him" (Psalm 18:30). He said, in effect, "Do you know that the Lord is infallible, perfect in all His ways? He is absolutely trustworthy and immovable, and therefore we can run to Him for shelter. He is a strong tower of refuge."

David opened this verse with a curious phrase, "This God" (Psalm 18:30). Israel was surrounded by nations full of idolatry and worship of false gods. God's people bore witness in the midst of other nations that there is only one true God. David was stating, "This is the one God, and there is no other. He is the God of love, truth, power, and mercy." This truth was important for Israel to remember because they were tempted at times to stray to the false gods around them.

We are no different today. False gods create false hope, so it's essential for the people of God to know Who He is. If you don't believe the Lord is faithful, you'll lead a life of fear. If you feel He isn't powerful, you won't believe He can break through your trials with victory. If you feel He's changeable, you'll live in fear that He may be kind to you one day but angry the next. Knowledge of God and His nature is essential to leading a breakthrough life.

WITHOUT A BREAKTHROUGH

A low view of God creates a low theology, low doctrine, and, as a result, an ineffective Christian life. A certain segment within the body of Christ teaches very little about God's nature other than He exists to fulfill our dreams and desires. To these churches, God is a genie to grant all our wishes, One Who is subservient to our passions and whims.

By contrast, theology that's true to God's nature reveals our own nature as sinful and selfish. This theology positions humankind where we belong, in need of a Savior. Once the church grasps an exalted view of God, we learn how to truly walk in worship. Such theology brings about true doxology, which is our song of God. We sing from a deep sense that our mourning can be broken, that grieving can end, and that victories can be won.

"This God—his way is perfect" (Proverbs 18:30). Here is one of the attributes of God: His perfection. God is impeccable, having no imperfections within Him. If we were able to view God from every angle,

His impeccable attributes would be present in each dimension: love, mercy, grace, justice, judgment, power, truth, and wisdom. Every one of his attributes is perfect.

When we think of perfections, we think of certain amazing things like a baby at birth or a wondrous sunset. Yet God's perfection is beyond anything we can think or imagine; it isn't capturable or measurable. David was saying in this verse, "If we want to have knowledge of God, then everything we understand about Him has to be through the lens of His perfection. His judgments are perfect. His justice is perfect. His love, mercy, and power are all perfect."

Another attribute of God is His faithfulness. "The word of the Lord proves true" (Psalm 18:30). If you ever doubt that what God says can be proven true, simply look back over your life. You'll see that everything He has done in you has proven to be perfectly true for what He has wanted to accomplish in you.

"And who is a rock, except our God?" (Psalm 18:31). The word *rock* speaks of a foundation, substance, an undergirding. We call this God's immutability or unchangeable nature. His every decree is perfectly reliable, creating a rock-solid foundation upon which we can lay our lives. Deuteronomy 32:31 reads, "For their rock is not as our Rock; our enemies are by themselves." Note the capitalization of "R" on *rock* in this verse. Only the Lord's foundation is perfect. No other people have the same undergirding that we do.

This truth was recognized by a non-Christian podcast host I once heard. One of my sons appeared on the show to speak about addictions and how we fight them. He has been free from his own addictions for many years; and as the host listened to him speak, he offered this realization: "I see that the difference between a Christian's recovery and a non-Christian's recovery is the sense of armor you have. You have a sense of protection." Even people who don't believe in Jesus can sense the difference.

THE LORD TRAINS OUR HANDS FOR WAR

The first type of equipping is to see Who God is; the second type is to see what God does. He is equipping us to fight death and the fear of it, to overcome it and to have victory. Psalm 18 lists multiple ways that God equips us to win a battle. Each way echoes the verse, "For by you I can run against a troop, and by my God I can leap over a wall" (Psalm 18:29). With these words—"by you" and "by my God"—David gave credit to the Lord that all victory, honor, and glory come through Him. Only by the hand of God are we given power to overcome the enemy.

So what are the things He empowers us to do? First, as David said, "I can run against a troop." The Hebrew word for *troop* here suggests a hostile band of marauders. We see this image in the story of Gideon, when food was hidden to protect it from passing marauders. Gideon knew that if the resources of God's people were found out, they would face famine.

David's counsel in Psalm 18 wasn't to hide but to attack. He said God empowers us to stand up and defeat every marauding enemy. He could testify to this because he personally faced literal bands of marauders.

> Now when David and his men came to Ziklag on the third day, the Amalekites had made a raid against the Negeb and against Ziklag. They had overcome Ziklag and burned it with fire and taken captive the women and all who were in it, both small and great. They killed no one, but carried them off and went their way. And when David and his men came to the city, they found it burned with fire, and their wives and sons

and daughters taken captive. Then David and the people who were with him raised their voices and wept until they had no more strength to weep. David's two wives also had been taken captive, Ahinoam of Jezreel and Abigail the widow of Nabal of Carmel. And David was greatly distressed, for the people spoke of stoning him, because all the people were bitter in soul, each for his sons and daughters. But David strengthened himself in the Lord his God (1 Sam. 30:1-6).

What a horrifying scene of captivity. Maybe you know forms of captivity in your life, perhaps sinful habits or thoughts of inadequacy, fear, doubt, or discouragement. I hear from Christians who say they can't get out of their backslidden state, others who say they're bound by selfish ambition, and others who say they're constantly driven by passions of the flesh. Multitudes feel helpless and hopeless in the face of their bondage.

David did not. He and his community were plundered by a marauding enemy, but he declared, "God has equipped and trained me to run against a troop." So what happened? "And David inquired of the Lord, 'Shall I pursue after this band? Shall I overtake them?' He answered him, 'Pursue, for you shall surely overtake and shall surely rescue'" (1 Sam. 30:8).

The rest of the story describes the victory God gave David and his men. When they came upon a young man from the enemy band, David grabbed him and demanded, "'Will you take me down to this band?'" (1 Sam. 30:15). In short, he was saying, "I want to go to the battle. Lord; let me run into this troop. Let me not be fearful or hold back, for You are my power."

I pray for each of us to be like David, wanting to be taken to the frontlines of battle against the ruler of this world. May we be willing for God to lead us to the fiercest places in society to do battle against the one who comes "'to kill, steal, and destroy'" (John 10:10). Evil is being perpetrated, and it needs to be cursed. As the people of God, we need the boldness to say, "This has to stop" and to move into action to make it happen.

Here was the result of God's equipping of David. "David recovered all that the Amalekites had taken, and David rescued his two wives. Nothing was missing, whether small or great, sons or daughters, spoil or anything that had been taken" (1 Sam. 30:18-19). When all seems lost, God restores everything that the enemy has taken. His direction to David, "You shall surely overtake," was all that David needed to hear. This same word is meant for us today.

PAUL'S LETTER TO THE EPHESIANS

Most Christians are familiar with the equipping Paul described in Ephesians 6:

> Finally, be strong in the Lord and in the strength of his might. Put on the whole armor of God, that you may be able to stand against the schemes of the devil. For we do not wrestle against flesh and blood, but against the rulers, against the authorities, against the cosmic powers over this present darkness, against the spiritual forces of evil in the heavenly places. Therefore take up the whole armor of God, that you may be able to withstand in the evil day, and having done all, to stand firm. Stand therefore, having fastened on the belt of truth, and having put on the breastplate of righteousness, and, as shoes for your feet, having put on the readiness given by the gospel of peace. In all circumstances take up the shield of faith, with which you can extinguish all the flaming darts of the evil one; and take the helmet of salvation, and the sword of the Spirit, which is the word of God, praying at all times in the Spirit, with all prayer and supplication (Eph. 6:10-18).

We understand the need for each of these weapons of warfare. Yet what good are such weapons if we never step into battle? Evil wages war all around us, against our flesh, against Christ's body, and through the gross darkness prevailing in the culture. There is a reason for the armor we're given: "that you may be able to stand against the schemes of the devil." Paul used multiple phrases throughout this passage to describe our marauding enemy: "the schemes of the devil," "cosmic powers," "spiritual forces of evil," "the flaming darts of the evil one." No matter what the battlefront, we are at war.

David spoke of two battlefronts. The first involves a troop; the second involves a wall. "For by you I can run against a troop, and by my God I can leap over a wall" (Psalm 18:29). The latter image is of a fortified city, which speaks of strongholds in our life. Before this, we were called to run into a troop. Now we're being called to scale impossible walls by the power of the Holy Spirit.

David knew he needed supernatural strength from the Lord in his real-life battles. In 2 Samuel 5, his enemies, the Jebusites, inhabited Jerusalem, which was protected by formidable walls. So when "the king (David) and his men went to Jerusalem against the Jebusites, the inhabitants of the land, who said to David, 'You will not come in here, but the blind and the lame will ward you off'—thinking, 'David cannot come in here'" (2 Sam. 5:6-7). The Jebusites taunted David, "This city is so fortified that even the lame and the blind can keep you out. You're helpless!"

They didn't realize the power that David had behind him. He retook Jerusalem through the Lord's power. "Nevertheless, David took the stronghold of Zion, that is, the city of David . . . And David lived in the stronghold and called it the city of David" (2 Sam. 5:7, 9). A few chapters later, David sang the victory song that would eventually appear in Psalm 18, word for word. "For by you I can run against a troop, and by my God I can leap over a wall" (2 Sam. 22:30).

The strongholds in our lives can seem powerfully fortified, walled in, impenetrable, and unscalable. They can overwhelm any sense of hope we have for combatting them. David spoke to our futility, advising us to look to the Lord's power, not our own. "By *you* . . . by *my God* . . ." (2 Sam. 22:30, my emphasis).

RUNNING AGAINST A TROOP AND LEAPING OVER A WALL

David testified, "For you equipped me with strength for the battle; you made those who rise against me sink under me" (Psalm 18:39). This echoes verse thirty-two: "The God who equipped me with strength." When it comes to being equipped, faith must enter in. We have to accept that God equips, trains, and empowers us for everything He calls us to do, from witnessing the lost to praying for the sick. These are the most basic commands of our calling, yet many have shrunk back from them. For these Christians, the battle is already lost because they never enter it.

David attached an interesting sentence to this verse about God equipping him: "and made my way blameless" (Psalm 18:32). This mention of blamelessness seems like a diversion from David's ongoing theme of warfare, yet it is embedded in the very center of a highly military sequence.

Warfare actually involves blamelessness and purity of heart. David was saying, "I am not distracted from the battle; I have total focus. I don't fall into traps of flesh. The Lord has shown me the right course of action, and I won't stray from it." David knew that the only way to go into battle was to be utterly attentive to the Lord's voice.

Time after time in David's military history, we see him seeking the Lord about whether to go into battle. This was a matter of course for him. It helped him plan his battles on the way to every victory God had planned for him. The same is true for us today. Our warfare requires prayer, asking, "Lord, I can't know how to fight this battle unless You show me Your heart. Teach me how to fight this enemy. You alone know the way through this conflict." The word for "blameless" in verse thirty-two is the same word in Hebrew that appears in verse thirty for "perfect." God has the perfect battle plan to bring you into His perfect victory for your life.

These twin processes of equipping and sanctification are joined together because our battle is spiritual. In Psalm 18, God takes us line by line, precept upon precept, through the process of how to lead a life that is increasingly holy. This, in turn, teaches us how to scale greater heights, giving us more victories over the enemy.

"He . . . set me secure on the heights" (Psalm 18:33). Once we're taken to the top of the wall, the picture is one of taking a stand. We are not to give up a single inch of ground we've taken. Let's say you had been backslidden, and now you've come back to the Lord. A familiar "sin . . . [crouches] at [your] door" (Gen. 4:7) and has begun tampering with your heart. Faith leads you to stand firm on that wall, taking a stance against the evil formed against you. God's strengthening grace empowers you to make that stand.

"He trains my hands for war, so that my arms can bend a bow of bronze" (Psalm 18:34). There are two ways to translate this verse. The first suggests hands and arms so stout that they're able to bend a bow made of inflexible material. A second translation, which I think is better, means hands and arms so strong that they actually *break* a bow made of bronze. This suggests taking an enemy's weapon and destroying it so that it no longer has power over you.

Imagine breaking your addiction into pieces or smashing a plaguing fear into bits. This would end all of the enemy's power over you. It's what God is training our hands to do for the sake of our soul, our marriage, our family, our church, and our community.

God also equips us by providing us with a shield and His right hand of support. "You have given me the shield of your salvation, and your right hand supported me" (Psalms 18:35). The image here is of protection from an advancing enemy, first by a shield and second by a mighty hand swooping down to do battle on our behalf. Picture the awesome image of God's hand appearing in the midst of your battle, taking hold of your enemies and making a quick end of them.

Next, God puts us in a "wide place." "You gave a wide place for my steps under me, and my feet did not slip" (Psalm 18:36). David was saying, "I'm steady now. I'm not wobbling wearily from my battles. I can see progress being made. Lord, you are bringing me into new victories!"

The last of the transformative ways God equips us to overcome our enemy is found in verse thirty-seven. "I pursued my enemies and overtook them, and did not turn back till they were consumed" (Psalm 18:37). This is not a partial victory but one that is complete and full. At this point, the attack against you doesn't come in the same form, say, as an addiction or despair. You are truly free. We will always face new battlefronts; but each time we can look back on the victories God has given us and testify, "I defeated that enemy. I overtook it and didn't turn my back until it was totally consumed. God has set me in a solid place."

WHEN HE EXALTS US

Not only does the Lord equip us with a knowledge of Him and by training our hands for war; He also equips us by exalting us. As I said before, this may sound strange to some of us, but Jesus told us, "'He who humbles himself will be exalted'" (Luke 14:11).

A huge part of God's work in the world is to reveal us as His shining workmanship. This may be the only explanation for why your marriage is still troubled, why you are constantly pulled by the lust of the world, or why you continue to be discouraged. You are in a trial because He is preparing to exalt you before the world as someone He has brought through the hardest trials of life. God is doing more than training you to defeat your enemies; He is showing His ability to transform a person who's in the most difficult circumstances. He is bringing you through your struggle to an exalted place for His Divine purposes.

Ultimately, here is what it means to be exalted: to be set free from the fear of defeat and death. For decades, I have seen the Lord exalt the lives of broken people who went through the Teen Challenge substance rehabilitation program. Everyone who entered this program, which my father founded, arrived in a state of defeat. Some had been near the brink of death through their addictions. Through the power of Jesus, they gained victory over their condition and the bondage that caused it. They are so transformed, set free, and filled with life that before long, they lead other broken souls to life. At this moment, in more than ninety countries throughout the world, there are powerful directors of Teen Challenge programs whose testimonies go beyond being set free; now they are leading scores of others to freedom.

These precious servants are so bold in their labors that they'll go into any dark corner to snatch a dying soul from Hell. They've seen their own lives resurrected by the power of the risen Christ, so now they fear nothing in their calling to rescue others. The Lord exalts them as powerful examples of His ability to restore the most heartrendingly broken lives.

ANOTHER FORM OF EXALTATION

"You delivered me from strife with the people" (Psalm 18:43). God elevates us from caustic strife that may plague our lives. He enables us to say, "You brought me out of conflicts with people that I thought would never end. You delivered me from all bitter contention and caused me to rise above it."

Again, David could testify about this from his own life. After Saul died and David ascended to the throne, restoring strength to Israel, Saul's family still had bitter resentments against him. Some tried to thwart his righteous rule. God turned all of that around. "And David grew stronger and stronger, while the house of Saul became weaker and weaker" (2 Sam. 3:1). The Lord makes our "house" strong while our enemies' power diminishes. We see our faith, our family, and our children grow stronger while our pain, sorrows, and struggles fade away.

David then exclaimed, "As soon as they heard of me they obeyed me; foreigners came cringing to me" (Psalm 18:44). This was not a boast. It was a real picture of the strength God bestows on those who allow themselves to be equipped for warfare. He brings us to a place where we can say, "Those who oppose me will continue to disagree with me, but the Holy Spirit will reveal the truth so that they are humbled before it."

The power and conviction that accompany God's presence and Word are seen throughout Scripture. Paul assumed this when he wrote, "All Scripture is breathed out by God and profitable for teaching, for reproof, for correction, and for training in righteousness" (2 Tim. 3:16). As we study God's Word and hear it preached, the Spirit breathes truth upon us, making it plain to our understanding and to nonbelievers' understanding as well. This same Divine power made truth known to the nonbelieving "foreigners" who cringed before David.

When Paul charged Timothy to preach the Word, it was to equip God's people with the knowledge of Him. "Preach the word; be ready in season and out of season; reprove, rebuke, and exhort, with complete patience and teaching" (2 Tim. 4:2). All of this was training for battle, powered by the conviction of the Spirit. The clarity of the gospel cuts through all confusion.

God's ways of equipping us for warfare—for battle, for victory, for overcoming the enemy—are seemingly endless. Each way prepares us for every good work He has planned for us.

TRAINING THAT LEADS TO WORSHIP

David wrapped up this lengthy, magnificent psalm on a note of praise. "For this I will praise you, O Lord, among the nations, and sing to your name. Great salvation he brings to his king, and shows steadfast love to his anointed, to David and his offspring forever" (Psalm 18:49-50). Note the word *anointed* in this passage. Ultimately, this psalm points out that our Savior is the One Who trains us. The ultimate triumph isn't ours over the devil; it is Christ's over the devil. All blessings come to us through His victory. By His authority, we see morning break after darkness and mourning turned into gladness. No matter what our battle or condition, we can wait on Jesus and know He will bring our breakthrough. He is the Righthand of the Father, Who brings victory in every area of our life—our health, our children, our job, our emotions, our relationships.

As we stand against the evil encroaching on the world, we don't face our enemies with arrogance or hatred. We always come in love. Our calling is to draw people out of the darkness, confusion, and ungodliness that separate them from God. In short, we are not against those who are caught in snares but against the one who ensnares them.

So know that as you patiently endure your struggle, Jesus is training and teaching you to run into battle, to bring you into a wide place, and to reveal you as His workmanship. You are going to see your trials crushed and your life exalted before others who need hope in their struggles. Your battles are bringing you to a new place of faith, confidence, joy, and victory so that you stand firm, secure, and unshakable on the Rock that is Christ.

CHAPTER TEN

Psalm 19
The Law of the Lord Is Perfect

1 The heavens declare the glory of God,
  and the sky above proclaims his handiwork.
2 Day to day pours out speech,
  and night to night reveals knowledge.
3 There is no speech, nor are there words,
  whose voice is not heard.
4 Their voice goes out through all the earth,
  and their words to the end of the world.
In them he has set a tent for the sun,
5   which comes out like a bridegroom leaving his chamber,
  and, like a strong man, runs its course with joy.
6 Its rising is from the end of the heavens,
  and its circuit to the end of them,
  and there is nothing hidden from its heat.
7 The law of the Lord is perfect,
  reviving the soul;
the testimony of the Lord is sure,
  making wise the simple;

8 the precepts of the Lord are right,
  rejoicing the heart;
the commandment of the Lord is pure,
  enlightening the eyes;
9 the fear of the Lord is clean,
  enduring forever;
the rules of the Lord are true,
  and righteous altogether.
10 More to be desired are they than gold,
  even much fine gold;
sweeter also than honey
  and drippings of the honeycomb.
11 Moreover, by them is your servant warned;
  in keeping them there is great reward.
12 Who can discern his errors?
  Declare me innocent from hidden faults.
13 Keep back your servant also from presumptuous sins;
  let them not have dominion over me!
Then I shall be blameless,
  and innocent of great transgression.
14 Let the words of my mouth and the meditation of my heart
  be acceptable in your sight,
  O Lord, my rock and my redeemer.

C.H. SPURGEON SAID OF THIS psalm, "The psalmist, while keeping his father's flock, had devoted himself to the study of God's two great books, one being nature, and the other being scripture." Psalm 19 celebrates both of these "books" of God. One is a book that speaks of God through creation, while the other speaks of Him through His literal Word. The first book gives us general revelation, which is found in God's handiwork: the sun, moon, stars, and earth below. The second book is God's specific revelation to us, His Word delivered.

Psalm 19 urges us to draw life from both books. Oftentimes, I gaze at my hand and think, "This is a miracle. My brain issues a command, and my hand obeys it." This is a simple thing, scientifically explained; but the beauty of the bodily system is a marvel beyond any that science could originate. I experience the same thing with babies. I have four children and nine grandchildren; and with each one born into the world, I marveled at the beauty of God's creation. His voice is so very clear through all of nature.

As incredible as these things are, however, the Lord speaks most importantly through the Scriptures, His loving Word to all of humankind. That is where David ultimately leads the reader in this powerful psalm.

DAVID LEARNED OF GOD

David seemed conscious of the things of God from his earliest years. He wrote in Psalm 139:

> For you formed my inward parts; you knitted me together in my mother's womb. I praise you, for I am fearfully and wonderfully made. Wonderful are your works; my soul knows it very well. My frame was not hidden from you, when I was being made in secret, intricately woven in the depths of the earth. Your eyes saw my unformed substance; in your book were written, every one of them, the days that were formed for me, when as yet there was none of them (Psalm 139:13-16).

David also probably learned God's ways during his upbringing. When the prophet Samuel showed up at his family's home, searching for the Lord's chosen king to rule Israel after Saul's disgrace, David was so young and small that his father didn't include him among the lineup of older brothers. "But the Lord said to Samuel, 'Do not look on his appearance or on the height of his stature, because I have rejected him. For the Lord sees not as man sees: man looks on the outward appearance, but the Lord looks on the heart'" (1 Sam. 16:7). Because David sought God with all his heart from an early age, the Lord directed Samuel to him over all his brothers.

As a mere boy tending his father's sheep in the fields and forests, David learned of God through his natural surroundings. The psalms he composed show a deep hunger to know more of God continually. Later, when David was anointed as king, he had access to the nation's treasury of knowledge about the Lord. This written knowledge was contained in the Torah, which is comprised of the first five books of the Bible. Deuteronomy tells us that all of Israel's kings were commanded to take these Scriptures and keep them on their body at all times.

> And when he sits on the throne of his kingdom, he shall write for himself in a book a copy of this law, approved by the Levitical priests. And it shall be with him, and he shall read in it all the days of his life, that he may learn to fear the Lord his God by keeping all the words of this law and these statutes, and doing them, that his heart may not be lifted up above his brothers, and that he may not turn aside from the commandment, either to the right hand or to the left, so that he may continue long in his kingdom, he and his children, in Israel (Deut. 17:18-20).

None of Israel's kings was permitted to go anywhere without their book but were to have it on hand to meditate on God's Word day and night. This would have delighted David, whose thoughts were on the Lord every moment of his life.

A MAN OF THE BOOK AND A HEART FOR THE BOOK

David's heart for the Lord didn't stop at composing and singing psalms of praise. His deep love for God's Word was included in his songs. He stated in Psalm 16, "I have set the Lord always before me; because he is at my right hand, I shall not be shaken" (Psalm 16:8). Having God at his right hand was literal for David. Rabbinical teachings tell us that kings would tie their little book of Scripture to their right hand and write in them testimonies, prayers, and meditations.

David held God's Word so close to his heart that when he was on his deathbed, he emphasized its importance to his son Solomon. "When David's time to die drew near, he commanded Solomon his son, saying, 'I am about to go the way of all the earth. Be strong, and show yourself a man, and keep the charge of the Lord your God, walking in his ways and keeping his statutes, his commandments, his rules, and his testimonies, as it is written in the Law of Moses, that you may prosper in all that you do and wherever you turn'" (1 Kings 2:1-3).

David's entire life revolved around God's Word. It was honored in his childhood home; as king, he carried it with him wherever he went. As an old man, he conveyed its centrality to life for the sake of future generations. He told Solomon, "Devour this Word. Hunger for it. Grow in it and speak it. Let the Word of the Lord be the highest pursuit of your life, above all other things."

The present generation of the Church needs a revival of God's Word. They need to see it taught, sung, preached, and proclaimed. In a sense, it should be tied to their right hand so that it remains before them at all times, available to refresh their soul.

A BREAK DOWN OF THESE TWO BOOKS OF GOD

In the opening section of this psalm, David pondered God's creation and general revelation. Then, in verses seven through nine, David spoke of God's specific revelation, meaning His Word. In the initial six verses, David used the word *El* or *Elohim* to speak of God. This particular name for the Lord means "sovereign" and "omnipotent." David was envisioning God as King, ruling from on high with power, majesty, and splendor. Then, in verses seven through nine, David switched gears and spoke of God's literal Word as His perfect law. The Hebrew word for God in these verses is *Yahweh*, which addresses the Lord more personally, as in a relationship. Altogether, through David's use of these two names, he was saying, "Elohim, I know something of Your power through Your creation. When I want to commune with You as a son to his father, I know You as Yahweh."

Invoking God's book of creation, David wrote, "The heavens declare the glory of God, and the sky above proclaims his handiwork" (Psalm 19:1). The word *heavens* speaks of lofty realms, such as the sky. As we look upward at the sun, moon, stars, and firmament, we see the handiwork of God. David said these say something important to us. In fact, his word *declare* is translated as the verb root "scribe," as in to inscribe or describe. He was saying that God's creation writes things into our understanding; it announces or preaches to us something to take in. What exactly is this message? David answered in the next part of the verse: "the glory of God." Simply put, nature reveals God's glory.

This is the point where the world falls short of understanding creation. People commune with nature all the time, seeking delight in the beauty of flowering trees, rippling ponds, trilling birdsong, or scurrying creatures. They leave a park or woods saying, "Nature is so glorious'"; but they've missed nature's message entirely. Every sway of a tree branch and every soaring bird proclaims the glory of God. All of these things preach Good News.

Despite God's voice being clear in natural wonders, people ignore it. Paul captured this tragic truth in a single verse. "For his invisible attributes, namely, his eternal power and divine nature, have been clearly perceived, ever since the creation of the world, in the things that have been made. So they are without excuse" (Rom. 1:20).

HUMILITY OR AUTONOMY

God never stops speaking through creation. "Day to day pours out speech, and night to night reveals knowledge" (Psalm 19:2). Nature not only declares God's glory, but it also pours out that message continually. One aspect of God's character is literally poured out from nature. I think of glowing lava flowing from volcanoes, mighty ocean waves pounding shores, torrential winds bending trees horizontal, things that Scripture sometimes calls the terrors of the Lord. These natural realities reflect the Creator's immense power, yet they are minuscule compared to His true omnipotence.

When we bring together all the verbs from these first few verses, we see nature declaring, which is preaching; proclaiming, which is letting others know; and pouring out speech, like a flowing fountain of knowledge. Simply put, nature is a preacher, proclaiming and revealing God without ceasing. This has been so since the beginning, and there isn't a place in all of creation where God's voice isn't heard. "There is no speech, nor are there words, whose voice is not heard" (Palm 19:3). Still, God's revelation is only partial through nature.

A FULLER, MORE SPECIFIC, AND LITERAL EXPRESSION OF GOD'S GLORY

A literal voice from Heaven would emerge in the latter days. Hebrews explains that this fullest expression of the Lord arrived in the form of His Son, Jesus. "Long ago, at many times and in many ways, God spoke to our fathers by the prophets, but in these last days he has spoken to us by his Son, whom he appointed the heir of all things, through whom also he created the world. He is the radiance of the glory of God and the exact imprint of his nature, and he upholds the universe by the word of his power" (Heb. 1:1-3). We behold God's nature and character through His creation, but Jesus Christ is God's profoundest expression of all.

In verses four through six, David invoked the image of the sun; but he easily could have been preaching about the Son. "Their voice goes out through all the earth, and their words to the end of the world. In them he has set a tent for the sun, which comes out like a bridegroom leaving his chamber, and, like a strong man, runs its course with joy. Its rising is from the end of the heavens, and its circuit to the end of them, and there is nothing hidden from its heat" (Psalm 19:4-6). Nothing under the sun is hidden from the rule and reign of the Father through the Son.

In this passage, it's as if David was presenting the image of the Son, a Bridegroom, coming forth to rule and reign over all creation. He was saying, in essence, "All the glories of nature pale compared to the greater light of glory found in the Son, the perfect embodiment of God's Word. Indeed, the sun in all its brilliance doesn't begin to approach the radiance of the Son in His glory."

David then made a sudden transition, shifting his focus from creation to God's Word. "The law (or Word) of the Lord is perfect, reviving the soul" (Psalm 19:7). Five more times in the next three verses (7b-9), David used the phrase "the Lord." "The testimony of the Lord is sure, making wise the simple; the precepts of the Lord are right, rejoicing the heart; the commandment of the Lord is pure, enlightening the eyes; the fear of the Lord is clean, enduring forever; the rules of the Lord are true, and righteous altogether" (Psalm 19:7-9).

David was saying, "All of these things are of the Lord—His law, His testimony, His precepts, His commandment, His rules, the fear of Him—and all are perfect." Note the verbs attached to these nouns: reviving, making wise, rejoicing, enlightening, enduring. Note also the descriptive words attached to them: perfect, sure, right, pure, clean, righteous. Altogether, these words comprise all that God's Word is and does. In total, they add up to a powerful prescription for a blessed life.

WORLDLY ANSWERS TO SPIRITUAL PROBLEMS

In Psalm 19, God responds to our misguided efforts, saying, "I have something for you that's perfect. It's my Word, and you have access to it at all times." Think about it: if your decisions are faulty, what's going to make you wise? "The testimony of the Lord is sure, making wise the simple" (Psalm 19:7). Your answer is found in God's testimony, which is His Word. It is "sure," according to David. He's saying, "The world offers you solutions that are far from perfect, but the wisdom found in God's Word is a sure thing." Simply put, we are to be like the prophet Jeremiah, who said, "Your words were found, and I ate them, and your words became to me a joy and the delight of my heart" (Jer. 15:16).

Do you lack joy? David claimed, "The precepts of the Lord are right, rejoicing the heart" (Psalm 19:8). In Hebrew, a precept is a guiding principle; and according to David, precepts bring joy. You may worry about being unhappy, thinking, "Maybe I need to see a counselor." Counselors can help, but God has a more direct solution for you: immerse yourself in His Word—read it, memorize it, get to know it—and you'll renew your knowledge of His love for you.

Do you feel like your life is in a fog, full of confusion? David prescribed, "The commandment of the Lord is pure, enlightening the eyes" (Psalm 19:8). His Word gives vision. All the trauma, heartache, and brokenness that's confusing you diminishes in the light of His truth. His Word makes your eyes shine brilliantly again.

His commands are pure, meaning unadulterated; they will not lead you astray. The fear of Him cleanses you, helping you to endure things with spiritual stamina. His rules are true and righteous altogether, meaning no part of them is false or lacking. Following them will not leave you hanging in any way.

IT IS TRUTH

We live in a culture where all truth is said to be relative. TV hosts constantly ask their guests, "Please, tell us your truth." Whenever I hear this, I want to throw a book at the screen. "Your" truth can lead you to leave your spouse simply because your life doesn't feel fulfilling. It can lead you to all kinds of damaging, destructive, flesh-driven decisions.

Unless we as a nation—and as a church—return to truth as truth, based on the Word of God, we'll be lost. As a young, insecure pastor, I used to want to leave people impressed by my sermons. That is no way to handle the Word of the Lord. Since then, the Holy Spirit has taught me to put my finger on a passage of Scripture and not lift it until I finish the sermon. This unyielding gesture keeps me focused, but it also conveys to everyone listening, "Don't look at me; look at the Word. Look at this book. Be a person of God's Word."

The Holy Spirit doesn't just make dreams and visions comes to pass; He makes us men and women of the Word, people who lead godly lives as a result. Ask Him to make the Word alive to you again. Let it become wisdom, life, and joy to you. Above all, thank Him that His Word is truth to live by. He has shown us His way; now let's walk in it.

CHAPTER ELEVEN

Psalm 20

Changing Lives Through Prayer

1 May the Lord answer you in the day of trouble!
  May the name of the God of Jacob protect you!
2 May he send you help from the sanctuary
  and give you support from Zion!
3 May he remember all your offerings
  and regard with favor your burnt sacrifices! *Selah*
4 May he grant you your heart's desire
  and fulfill all your plans!
5 May we shout for joy over your salvation,
  and in the name of our God set up our banners!
May the Lord fulfill all your petitions!
6 Now I know that the Lord saves his anointed;
  he will answer him from his holy heaven
  with the saving might of his right hand.
7 Some trust in chariots and some in horses,
  but we trust in the name of the Lord our God.
8 They collapse and fall,
  but we rise and stand upright.
9 O Lord, save the king!
  May he answer us when we call.

PSALM 20 MARKS A MAJOR shift in what we've read to this point. This psalm shows how David transitioned from praying for himself to praying for others, and his example demonstrates how this can happen in our lives as well. We've already seen that when we petition Heaven with our requests, God does not sit idle; this also holds true of our prayers for others. He won't neglect our intercession; to stay on the sidelines is not in His nature. He is full of mercy, grace, kindness, and love; and that brings us great hope through every trial.

Most of the themes we read in the first few Psalms continue through Psalm 17. These are about David in turmoil, trials, and troubles; and we saw his need for a breakthrough to deliverance. He cried out to God again and again, "How long, O Lord?"

Then in Psalm 18, we saw a transition begin to take place. David spoke of God having rescued him from his enemies, and he opened the Psalm by declaring, "I love you, O Lord" (Psalm 18:1). Something major had happened not only in David's circumstances but also in his understanding. He realized, in effect, "God heard me when my prayers rose to Him, and He stood up and delivered me." Two verses later, David gave us the basic template for effectual praying. "I call upon the Lord, who is worthy to be praised, and I am saved from my enemies" (Psalm 18:3). At its core, this statement is about acting in faith and the belief that God is faithful to move on our behalf.

At that point in his life, David had begun to see breakthroughs; and he celebrated by seeking the Lord in a more passionate way. This helped him to recognize God's ways as evident everywhere he looked. In Psalm 19, which Scripture titles, "The Law of the Lord Is Perfect," David wrote that the heavens and the earth declare the glory of God.

All of this drove him to know more of the Lord and His Word. He said, in effect, "I thank God for all my deliverances. He has blessed me beyond measure, and that gives me power to pray with confidence. Now, after everything He has done for me, I want to see others have breakthroughs like mine. I want their lives to be blessed by God in the ways I've been blessed. All of His promises are confirmed in His Word, and they are available to everyone facing trials and tribulations. So, as I seek Him in prayer, I will petition Him to move on behalf of others, too."

David spelled out all of this in a glorious way in the opening verses of Psalm 20.

> May the Lord answer you in the day of trouble! May the name of the God of Jacob protect you! May he send you help from the sanctuary and give you support from Zion! May he remember all your offerings and regard with favor your burnt sacrifices! *Selah* May he grant you your heart's desire and fulfill all your plans! May we shout for joy over your salvation, and in the name of our God set up our banners! May the LORD fulfill all your petitions! (Psalm 20:1-5).

David had learned what God could do for him. Now he wanted the people of God to know what He could do for them. He was claiming, "We all have the same power to call down Heaven's blessings. What God has done for me, He will do for you!"

THE PRIVILEGE OF PETITIONING THE LORD

If you have walked with Jesus for any length of time, you've seen God stop the attacks of enemies and deliver you from evil. I can testify to this.

God's love reached all of my prodigal children and brought them home after years in the wilderness. The Lord set me free from my own sinful patterns. He delivered me from cancer. After a serious car accident, He healed me of a broken back when I wasn't sure I would ever walk again. Through all of this, He set me on the solid Rock of His Word, building my confidence that all my prayers reach and move Him.

In this context, Psalm 20 contains three themes I want to examine. The first theme is help in overcoming our troubles. The second theme is reward for our sacrifice. The third theme is the fulfillment of our heart's desires.

To begin, let's look at an important key in verse six. It's a brief phrase of only three words: "Now I know" (Psalm 20:6). In previous psalms, David cried, "How long, O Lord?" Here in Psalm 20, he answered his own question. He was on the other side of deliverance, and he testified, "Now I know that the LORD saves his anointed; he will answer him from his holy heaven with the saving might of his right hand" (Psalm 20:6).

Before this, David wasn't so sure that the Lord was listening to his petitions. Now he knew God had been listening all along. That is the crux of this chapter: "Now I know!" This sort of powerful revelation moves us to pray for others to have the same experience: "Our marriage was in trouble, but He rescued us. Now I know He'll do the same for other couples." "My children were lost, but He saved them. Now I know He'll do the same for other prodigals." "He set me free from sin. Now I know He can set others free, too." "I know that all He has done for me, He will do for others, too."

I urge every Christian to have these three words burning in their heart and mind: *Now I know.* I know what God will do because I know what He has already done. I can pray for others with confidence because I know He'll move in their lives like He did in mine. I know the Lord hears our cries!" If you cling to this conviction, you can trust you'll see changes in others' lives. They'll testify to you about it, and you can urge them to pray for others in turn. Thus begins a holy cycle in Christ's body flowing continually outward with deliverance that sets person after person free.

THE POWERFUL REQUESTS DAVID MADE FOR OTHERS IN THIS PSALM

"May the Lord answer you in the day of trouble . . . protect you . . . send you help . . . give you support . . . remember all your offerings . . . regard with favor your burnt sacrifices . . . grant you your heart's desire . . . fulfill all your plans! May we shout for joy over your salvation, and . . . (m)ay the Lord fulfill all your petitions!" (Psalm 20:1-5).

These prayers for others might seem simple, but they are deeply profound. All of David's "mays" in this list were blessings he had experienced for himself, and you have your own as well. Who among us isn't thrilled to shout, "Lord, You answered me! You sent help. You protected me. Your mercies really do endure forever"? If these joys aren't enough to move you to prayer for others, nothing will.

There was a time in your life when someone somewhere prayed for you faithfully. Maybe it was a loving grandmother, a distant relative who loved Jesus, a good friend who stuck "closer than a brother" (Prov. 18:24), or maybe even a child. At age twelve, my wife, Kelly, was the first in her family to come to Jesus. She immediately began praying for her father, a navy veteran who was a gruff, swearing sort of guy. Eventually, he came to faith, as did the rest of Kelly's family; and it all began with the prayers of an adolescent girl. Kelly knows firsthand that the simplest, most childlike prayers we offer for others are heard by God and that He answers them as faithfully as He does for the most devoutly praying saint. He comes to the side of every Christian with life-changing power.

"May he send you help from the sanctuary and give you support from Zion!" (Psalm 20:2). Zion is the city of God that David retook from the Jebusites. When the Israelites conquered the city, they cried out, "May we shout for joy over your salvation, and in the name of our God set up our banners!" (Psalm 20:5). They raised up flags around the city walls, signifying that the Lord ruled over their lives.

We can do the same with our marriage, our children, and every aspect of our lives, planting God's flag of rule over everything concerning us. Note also a phrase in verse two: "May he send you help from the sanctuary" (Psalm 20:2). This speaks of the temple, where God's presence dwelled. So we have protection not only from the walls He erects around us but also from His presence, where we receive His mercy and grace.

Of course, God sends us help from above as well. "He will answer him from his holy heaven" (Psalm 20:6). All the resources of Heaven are available to us when we call on Him. He opens His treasuries to everyone who petitions on behalf of others. David was telling us in the verse, "Lord, open up your storehouses to your children. Let them know the riches of your knowledge and wisdom and revelation that they might know the glory of your ways."

There is another telling phrase in this last verse: "the saving might of his right hand" (Psalm 20:6). This is an image of God's omnipotence and power on our behalf. His purposes for us simply can't be stopped. So when you're praying for others, you can know the Lord's strength for them will not be turned back. He will fulfill every dimension of his will.

All of this happens in the name of the Lord, a phrase that appears three times within the psalm's nine verses. This speaks to the faithful reliability of God's nature. There are many Hebrew names for God, each beginning with Jehovah and each describing a distinct character trait, such as "God heals"; "God delivers"; "God is everlasting"; "God shows mercy." Even His name builds confidence in His faithfulness.

HOW THE LORD HELPS US OVERCOME OUR TROUBLES

David made an important assumption when he opened Psalm 20: "May the Lord answer you in the day of trouble!" (Psalm 20:1). He knew that all who love the Lord are going to face troubled days. This is a proven reality. However, when David prayed for God to "answer" us, he wasn't stating that our circumstances will always change. Instead, the Hebrew word suggests a meaning closer to "respond" or "get back to you." In other words, God's "answer" may be, "I see you in your desperate trial, and I bear the pain with you."

When we cry to God with the most pressing issues of our lives, He is not unmoved; He hears us. Even if our circumstances don't change, we can know He stands with us to help us endure our difficulty. Sometimes, His voice is enough. The apostle Paul addressed this beautifully in a passage that has encouraged suffering Christians for over two millennia. He wrote:

> A thorn was given me in the flesh, a messenger of Satan to harass me, to keep me from becoming conceited. Three times I pleaded with the Lord about this, that it should leave me. But he said to me, "My grace is sufficient for you, for my power is made perfect in weakness." Therefore I will boast all the more gladly of my weaknesses, so that the power of Christ may rest upon me. For the sake of Christ, then, I am content with weaknesses, insults, hardships,

persecutions, and calamities. For when I am weak, then I am strong (2 Cor. 12:7-10).

This passage ought to bring the church to its collective knees in gratitude. I urge every reader to embrace the Lord's glorious promise here: "My grace is sufficient for you" (2 Cor. 12:9). Sometimes, our answer from God isn't a change in our circumstances. Many who prayed desperately for healing in their marriage saw it end in divorce. Some who are sick don't recover, despite fervent prayers. The point of Paul's experience is not that a thorn remains in our flesh; it is that no matter what we face, we have grace to face it. Despite deep anguish and pain, there is joy knowing that the Lord stands with us through everything.

When David wrote of trouble in verse one, the Hebrew root carries a meaning of "narrow, meager, anxious." This speaks of being in a narrow strait, hemmed in without sufficient means to survive. So when our circumstances overwhelm us, causing anxiety, we can know God hears our cry and gives us grace sufficient for our need.

According to both Paul and David, each of us can say, *"Now I know* that the Lord doesn't just give us grace to endure. No matter how the storm may rage, He is doing the best thing possible for me. I know He is good, faithful, and holy; and that brings peace to my soul."

In the second half of the opening verse, David added, "May the name of the God of Jacob protect you!" (Psalm 20:1). Here, David moved from the subject of God's presence to God's protection. This is clear from his mention of Jacob. David was reminding his listeners of the episode from history when Jacob had to face his threatening brother, Esau. Jacob had deceived Esau out of his birthright; and years later, Esau pursued him with an army that could have meant Jacob's death. Instead, when Esau overcame Jacob, he cried with him and blessed him. It was a surprising grace, to say the least.

Some of the pain we go through ends up strengthening us. It builds our dependency on the Lord to trust Him with our thorn in the flesh, even when it looks like the end of our flesh. This leads to the next verse: "May he send you help from the sanctuary and give you support from Zion!" (Psalm 20:2). The word *send* in Hebrew means to let loose or open up the windows of Heaven and release God's resources. In this sense, sending doesn't indicate, "The check is in the mail" but that the check is already in your hands because it comes straight from Heaven's storehouse.

How are we to receive this support? First, we accept that it is ours; God says it is. Second, we accept that it has been sent to us from Him. Third, we accept that we already possess it, that it is in our hands. Fourth, we accept that it comes from a place that is holy and good and therefore can be trusted. Fifth, we accept that the source, Heaven's storehouse, is never closed to us. All of this is worth rejoicing over.

THE LORD REWARDS OUR SACRIFICE

David wrote, "May he remember all your offerings and regard with favor your burnt sacrifices!" (Psalm 20:3). No one merits God's favor; that's impossible. At the same time, though, David assured, "If you seek him, he will be found by you" (1 Chron. 28:9). This is not a condition as much as it is a cause and effect. For example, if you pray, God will answer you; whereas if you don't pray, how can you hear from Him? At the same time, if you offer the Lord a sacrifice of praise, you can know He will hear it and honor it.

Jesus told us, "'Give, and it will be given to you. Good measure, pressed down, shaken together, running over, will be put into your lap. For with the measure you use it will be measured back to you'" (Luke 6:38). Paul echoed this, writing, "Knowing that whatever good anyone does, this he will receive back from the Lord" (Eph. 6:8).

This is what David was saying. "Lord, do you remember all the times your people praised you when they were surrounded by trouble? Remember their sacrifices of faith, time, energy, and resources. You will not forget them, Lord. Your people will know Your mercy and kindness, and You will increase it to them as never before."

THE LORD FULFILLS ALL OUR HEART'S DESIRES

David wrote, "May he grant you your heart's desire and fulfill all your plans!" (Psalm 20:4). This seems almost too good to be true. Was this just exuberance on David's part? How could it possibly be real?

As we look at the original Hebrew, the word for *desires* is not plural but singular. Therefore, *desires* doesn't mean, "I want a house and car and wife and family." Instead, it is a singular desire, as when David wrote in a later psalm, "*One thing have I asked* of the Lord, that will I seek after: that I may dwell in the house of the Lord all the days of my life, to gaze upon the beauty of the Lord and to inquire in his temple" (Psalm 27:4, my emphasis).

David wasn't saying, "Don't dare ask for anything other than this," or, "Don't pray for your family or your health." Rather, he was saying, "All of these blessings come out of a single desire." This is the essence of Jesus's teaching, "Therefore do not be anxious, saying, 'What shall we eat?' or 'What shall we drink?' or 'What shall we wear?' For the Gentiles seek after all these things, and your heavenly Father knows that you need them all. But seek first the kingdom of God and his righteousness, and all these things will be added to you" (Matt. 6:31-33).

We've been talking about desires in verse four; but in the Hebrew here, the word *desires* isn't literally present. The verse actually reads, "May he grant you your heart." This echoes Jesus' teaching that "out of the abundance of the heart the mouth speaks" (Matt. 12:34). In other words, what is present in your heart will come out; and this includes your desires. So when you pray, is it only for personal success and material goods? Or do you pray as Paul did for one thing: "For I decided to know nothing among you except Jesus Christ and him crucified" (1 Cor. 2:2)?

On the other hand, sometimes we have holy desires; but they're too small for what God wants to accomplish through us. He told Isaiah, "It is too light a thing that you should be my servant to raise up the tribes of Jacob and to bring back the preserved of Israel; I will make you as a light for the nations, that my salvation may reach to the end of the earth" (Isa. 49:6). God was telling the prophet, "You desire to bring back My people to the land, but I want to do more. I want to make Israel a light shining outward to the nations, a beacon that beams forth the power of My salvation." If you give God your desires, He won't allow them to be diminished. He will instead refine and increase them, bringing glory to Himself and more joy to your heart than you could ever imagine.

So what happens then? We raise up banners of victory in His name. We declare that He is present in our midst and that His protective covering is a reality in our lives. As David wrote in a later Psalm, "Let me dwell in your tent forever! Let me take refuge under the shelter of your wings" (Psalm 61:4). God's banner of protection is both temporal and eternal.

It flew over Jerusalem, the holy city; and it's going to fly over the New Jerusalem, the everlasting city that will come down from Heaven.

This is all meant to build our trust. As David said in verse seven, "Some trust in chariots and some in horses, but we trust in the name of the Lord our God" (Psalm 20:7). This brings up Old Testament images, recalling certain kings of Israel who were tempted to ask idolatrous nations to help them against attacks by greater powers. David was warning against this, saying, "The people of God have no other source than God."

When we're in physical pain, we can go to a doctor for medicine; and when we're in financial stress, we can go to a banker for a loan. But our ultimate Source for all things is the Lord. Institutions collapse and fall, but the Lord will sustain His people. "They collapse and fall, but we rise and stand upright" (Psalm 20:8).

Do you feel like your life is going to collapse? Do you fear the failure of your finances or your health? God is telling you not to trust in chariots, the world, or your own power. "Trust in the Lord with all your heart, and do not lean on your own understanding. In all your ways acknowledge him, and he will make straight your paths" (Prov. 3:5-6).

The verse David chose to close Psalm 20 is interesting. In this verse, we see a reversal in the narrator. After eight verses of David praying for the people, it's as if the whole nation were given the chance to pray for King David. "O Lord, save the king! May he answer us when we call" (Psalm 20:9). This may have been a way of saying, "David, may God remember all the offerings you made for us and bless you in return. May the requests that you made for us on your knees, in the middle of the night, now fall back on you."

So the cycle continues. As an ever-increasing number of saints pray outwardly for others, they end up blessed themselves.

THE KIND AND GENEROUS NATURE OF GOD

David was saying in this Psalm, "Lord, You have given me such rich blessings. I asked You for life, and You gave me length of days. When I prayed for a breakthrough, You sent me many deliverances. I prayed for others, and the blessings that came upon them have now returned to me."

Through this Psalm, David showed us the powerful promises that await us and others. As we pray for those in need, we know these requests will be answered. We'll see people healed and delivered; and in the process, we will receive blessings ourselves. That is the goodness of our God.

CHAPTER TWELVE

Psalm 21
The Favor and the Fire of Jesus

1 O Lord, in your strength the king rejoices,
  and in your salvation how greatly he exults!
2 You have given him his heart's desire
  and have not withheld the request of his lips. *Selah*
3 For you meet him with rich blessings;
  you set a crown of fine gold upon his head.
4 He asked life of you; you gave it to him,
  length of days forever and ever.
5 His glory is great through your salvation;
  splendor and majesty you bestow on him.
6 For you make him most blessed forever;
  you make him glad with the joy of your presence.
7 For the king trusts in the Lord,
  and through the steadfast love of the Most High
he shall not be moved.
8 Your hand will find out all your enemies;
  your right hand will find out those who hate you.
9 You will make them as a blazing oven
  when you appear.

> The Lord will swallow them up in his wrath,
>   and fire will consume them.
> 10 You will destroy their descendants from the earth,
>   and their offspring from among the children of man.
> 11 Though they plan evil against you,
>   though they devise mischief, they will not succeed.
> 12 For you will put them to flight;
>   you will aim at their faces with your bows.
> 13 Be exalted, O Lord, in your strength!
>   We will sing and praise your power.

THE TITLE OF THIS CHAPTER speaks of two elements integral to who Jesus is: favor and fire. Verses one through seven speak of His favor, or grace, which He won for us on the cross. Verses eight through twelve speak of His fire, which is the ultimate reality for those who refuse His favor. Both are central to Who the Lord is.

In the previous Psalm, we found David praying for his people. The ending verse of that Psalm read, "O Lord, save the king! May he answer us when we call" (Psalm 20:9). King David had been praying for the people; but in that final verse, the people prayed in turn for God to bless their king. In short, the requests that David made for others were now being prayed for him. It's a beautiful picture of God's favor coming back on those who request it for others.

Scholars and commentaries tell us that many of the Psalms are understood not only through a Davidic lens but also a Christ-centric lens. In other words, a prayer of David in a Psalm may also be Jesus's prayer. That is true of Psalm 21, as well as the one that follows. In fact, we'll see this in the next chapter, on Psalm 22, where David cried, "My God, my

God, why have you forsaken me?" (Psalm 22:1). Of course, we know these words are Christ's cry from the cross in Matthew 27:46 and Mark 15:34. However, Jesus wasn't quoting David with this cry. On the contrary, in Psalm 22, David was prophesying that these would be the words Jesus would cry from the cross.

Psalm 22 contains other echoes of prophecy about the crucifixion, such as, "I am poured out like water, and all my bones are out of joint" (Psalm 22:14). In fact, the final four words of Psalm 22—"He has done it"—can be read as Jesus' final words from the cross, "It is finished" (John 19:30).

In these ways, Psalm 22 is a psalm of Jesus as well as a psalm of David. The same is true of Psalm 21, which is this chapter's topic. Whereas Psalm 22 prophesied suffering and being forsaken and a declaration of Christ's finished work, Psalm 21 prophesied what happened before the cross, notably the covenant between Jesus and the Father. It tells of the plan that the Father had for the Son, saying, "Here is what you will do."

CHRIST'S FAVOR (VV. 1-7)

David opened Psalm 21 by writing, "O Lord, in your strength the king rejoices, and in your salvation how greatly he exults!" (Psalm 21:1). The Hebrew word for *salvation* here is Yeshua, which signifies both Joshua in the Old Testament and also Jesus. In other words, King David rejoiced at the thought of what the Son would accomplish by the Father's strength. This accomplishment, of course, was the saving work of Yeshua embodied in the Savior Jesus.

As I mentioned, Psalm 21 finds Jesus before the crucifixion. Incredibly, He rejoiced at facing the cross, yet this was because He knew what that work would accomplish. Despite the suffering He faced—having the sins of the world laid fully on him, as well as the full wrath of God—Jesus knew the glorious result it would bring. He would become the Inheritance of the nations; the Father would give Him many children; and He would bring forth the gift of salvation that has blessed generations for two thousand years.

No one's suffering compares to that of Jesus's on the cross; yet at times, many of us feel like crying out, "God, why have you forsaken me?" I know I have. This psalm addresses our cry, telling us that we can do as Jesus did: We can face our suffering knowing salvation is real and that His work for us is finished. Even if we still face difficulty, His completed work will accomplish its purposes in our lives.

"You have given him his heart's desire and have not withheld the request of his lips" (Psalm 21:2). We have already discussed that Jesus's desire was singular. Again, I have to point out how different our desires are from his. Sadly, the way a lot of Christians move through life is with selfishness. Multitudes have a "me" mentality that asks, "What will I get out of this?" This question even applies to serving God.

The verse above in Psalm 21 cuts directly against this approach. Jesus' heart's desire was all for our benefit. That is why I would rather see His heart's desire fulfilled in my life than my own lofty desires, which are miniscule and fleshly in comparison. Even at my best, my desires can be worldly. I want less suffering and difficulty, so I seek comfort and not sacrifice.

Thankfully, Jesus won't give us our fleshly desires. Consider His question: "'Or which one of you, if his son asks him for bread, will give him a stone? Or if he asks for a fish, will give him a serpent?'" (Matt. 7:9). I would like to reverse this and ask, "If you ask for a snake, do you think Jesus would give it to you?" No, he won't; but the world will. The Lord gives good gifts. "'If you then, who are evil, know how to give good gifts to your children, how much more will your Father who is in heaven give good things to those who ask him'" (Matt. 7:10-11).

So, what was Jesus' heart's desire that David referred to in this psalm? Jesus told us directly in John 17, with three powerful words: "'Father, I desire'" (John 17:24). Almost the entire chapter of John 17 is comprised of Jesus' prayer for us. Here was his first request: "And this is eternal life, that they know you, the only true God, and Jesus Christ whom you have sent" (John 17:3). The fact that we could know God at all is an awesome reality, and it happened through the covenant the Father made with the Son. In fact, your act of reading this right now is likely the result of His salvation being a reality in your life.

The second thing Jesus prayed for us is, "'And I am no longer in the world, but they (we) are in the world, and I am coming to you. Holy Father, keep them in your name, which you have given me'" (John 17:11). Jesus was praying for our protection that the Father would keep us from worldliness and apostasy. Even though we are followers of Christ, a downfall into temptation is still a possibility; thus, Jesus asked the Father to keep us in His name.

So it's easy to see why Psalm 21 says, "In your strength the king rejoices" (Psalm 21:1). David knew that when we come to the Father, we can know we're protected by the greatest strength of all, supplied by the one and only King. We don't have to live in fear or doubt because "he who began a good work in you will bring it to completion at the day of Jesus Christ" (Phil. 1:6).

Jesus also prayed for unity with each other as well as with the Father and Son "'that they may be one, even as we are one'" (John 17:9). He added a prayer for us to be filled with joy. "'But now I am coming to you, and these things I speak in the world, that they may have my joy fulfilled in themselves'" (John 17:13). No matter what is happening around us or within us, if we are one with the Son, the Father, and one another, we will have joy.

He then prayed for our protection from the wiles of the devil. "'I do not ask that you take them out of the world, but that you keep them from the evil one'" (John 17:15). Satan is constantly plotting, scheming, and laying traps for us. None of these will prosper, though, because Jesus has asked the Father to keep us from them.

"'Sanctify them in the truth; your word is truth'" (John 17:17). Being sanctified by God's Word removes the world's stain from us and breaks our habitual sin patterns. If we want to become more and more like Jesus, we have to know this happens through understanding truth: "As Christ loved the church and gave himself up for her, that he might sanctify her, having cleansed her by the washing of water with the word, so that he might present the church to himself in splendor" (Eph. 5:25-27).

Something powerful and profound is released when we immerse ourselves in God's Word. "How can a young man keep his way pure? By guarding it according to your word" (Psalm 119:9). As I read this, I pray for a renewed passion for the scriptures. If you sense a similar hunger stirring in your soul, it is because the Father is answering Jesus's prayer for you.

Finally, Jesus prayed, "'Father, I desire that they also, whom you have given me, may be with me where I am, to see my glory that you have given me because you loved me before the foundation of the world'" (John 17:24). Christ was saying, "Father, let them be with Me in the eternal glory I have received from You. Bring them into everlasting life so that they can behold Your glory in its fullness." Consider all that Jesus has prayed for us in John 17. If you were to spend your lifetime rereading this chapter, how could your heart not be overwhelmed with joy and thanksgiving over all that Jesus prays for you continually?

HOW JESUS' PRAYERS WORK IN OUR LIVES

Jesus knew that Peter was going to be tempted terribly by Satan, so He prayed for him. "'Simon, Simon, behold, Satan demanded to have you, that he might sift you like wheat, but I have prayed for you that your faith may not fail. And when you have turned again, strengthen your brothers'" (Luke 22:31-32).

Note the type of sin that Peter was subjected to in this particular temptation: apostasy. Satan wants more than just to trip us up; he leads us into particular types of evil in order to destroy our faith. He wants no less than to take possession of our lives. What is Jesus' answer to this? "'I have prayed for you that your faith may not fail'" (Luke 22:32). Peter ended up denying Jesus three times; but the good news is that no matter how many times we fail, Christ won't leave us alone in our failure because He keeps praying for us continually. He's telling us, "I have you in the palm of My hand, and no devil or human can snatch you out."

Jesus' prayers are always answered. So even after Peter's repeated denials of the Lord, Christ raised him up to be a man of God who would "'feed [His] sheep'" (John 21:15-17). Jesus does the same with us. I receive emails from a lot of people who say, "My sin has overwhelmed me, and I feel like I'm losing my salvation." If this describes you, understand that Jesus has prayed for you and that not one of His prayers fails. He is praying that, like Peter, you'll pass through this season of trial and come out on the other side freed by His grace and sanctified by His Word.

"'And when you have turned again'" (Luke 22:32). Whenever we fail, we are to turn again to Him because He has not given up on us. We'll see Christ's face and know He has been waiting for us, never forsaking us. Our confidence will be renewed in His never-ending work in us.

I love that Jesus didn't say, "*If* you turn again." He never demands, "If you feel sorry enough, if you make enough promises to Me, if you plead with Me, then I'll be here for you." No, He said, "*When* you turn again," with no other condition. This implies that He takes up the work from that moment. That work is His acceptance, cleansing, transformation, and approval. I urge you, trust in the strength of the King. You can rejoice in it. I pray your "when" happens today.

WHAT JESUS PRAYS FOR YOU

The book of Hebrews says Jesus made an oath never to change His mind. "The Lord has sworn and will not change his mind, 'You are a priest forever. This makes Jesus the guarantor of a better covenant" (Heb. 7:21). The things that Jesus prays for us are continually being brought before the Father because they made an oath that His prayers are both yes and amen for our lives.

John 17 was Jesus' high priestly prayer; and Hebrews 7 confirms His work as High Priest, ever interceding for us in the Father's presence. His "better covenant" includes salvation, sanctification, protection, unity, joy, and protection from evil. As we turn and draw near to Him, these are His incredible gifts that transform our lives.

"Consequently, he is able to save to the uttermost those who draw near to God through him, since he always lives to make intercession for them" (Heb. 7:25). "Uttermost" speaks of the depth and breadth of His affection for us and His effectiveness in our lives. Moreover, the covenant oath between the Father and Son ensures that every request and intercession made for you will be granted. So when Jesus asks it, the Father agrees to it; and it is immediately released in your life. It may not seem to you that the promise has come—that, say, you still don't have joy in your heart—but His work is continual; and it is guaranteed. The promise won't be withheld; it will be accomplished.

This should bring you peace. To paraphrase the great Scottish preacher Robert Murray McCheyne, "If I could hear Christ praying for me in the next room, I would not fear a million enemies." I can relate to this. When I was a boy and my father was home from his frequent ministry travels, at night, he would come into the bedroom I shared with my younger brother to pray with us. He would kneel at the side of our bed, hold our hands, and pray, "Father, protect them. Show them Your love. Keep them in Your Word. Give them a hunger for You. Let the call of God be upon their lives. Use them mightily."

I knew that my father was a godly man, and merely hearing him pray these words gave me peace and confidence. Nothing that he prayed for happened immediately; but I knew even at that age that whatever he prayed, the Lord would hear. How much more is this so when Jesus prays for us?

THE VICTORY JESUS WON FOR US

An interesting truth is embedded in David's verse: "For you meet him with rich blessings; you set a crown of fine gold upon his head" (Psalm 21:3). The Hebrew word for *meet* here strangely appears in the King James Version as "preventest." To us, the word *prevent* means to stop something before it happens. In this biblical passage, though, it means "prevenient" or "going before." Here is what that means for us in this context.

Even before Jesus prayed in John 17, the Father knew what he would pray. Unprevented by time, the Lord's salvation moved to bless those in earlier times who looked forward to the coming of the Messiah and the event that would establish His salvation. The Father promised these faithful ones, in essence, "To anyone who cherishes the day when My Son accomplishes salvation on the cross, I will grant the same grace as to those who receive His work after it is finished."

So the merits of Christ were graced to those who came before and believed. "These all died in faith, not having received the things promised, but having seen them and greeted them from afar" (Heb. 11:13). These saints were looking toward a distant land, knowing that the promise wasn't in land or buildings or anything material and, therefore, passing; but that what to come was eternal. Today, we can look back to see Christ's finished work, both in Scripture and in history, achieved two thousand years ago and enduring through time and beyond it. We also see in Christ's High Priestly prayer the timeless power and beauty of the better covenant he made.

THE AUTHORITY IN THE CROWN ON KING JESUS' HEAD

David wrote, "You set a crown of fine gold upon his head" (Psalm 21:3). Christ's crown is secure, established, and will never be removed. We can read of the rise and fall of powerful Roman emperors and people like Alexander the Great, but Christ's authority never fades. None of those earthly figures could give life, but David wrote of the Father,

"He asked life of you; you gave it to him, length of days forever and ever" (Psalm 21:4). The Father gave the Son His own everlasting life. "'For as the Father has life in himself, so he has granted the Son also to have life in himself'" (John 5:26). In turn, Jesus passed on eternal life to us: "'Because I live, you also will live'" (John 14:19).

"His glory is great through your salvation; splendor and majesty you bestow on him" (Psalm 21:5). The Hebrew word for glory in this verse is *kavad*, meaning in biblical terms "to weigh heavily on." This suggests weightiness or what we call *grativas*, meaning substance. The word *splendor* here evokes an awe of beauty, as in the perfect diamond, a beautiful gem that amazes by its color, size, and clarity.

"For you make him most blessed forever; you make him glad with the joy of your presence" (Psalm 21:6). The two sentences that make up this verse form an image of the incomparable Christ. First, He is most blessed, being higher than angels and Moses and Elijah. He is the Word of Life Himself, higher than anything at all. Second, His happiness comes from the joy of the Father's constant presence, and He prays that we share that joy "'that they may have my joy fulfilled in themselves'" (John 17:13). Not only is Jesus the most blessed forever, but He is also the Source of all blessed joy.

"Through the steadfast love of the Most High he shall not be moved" (Psalm 21:7). Even knowing his impending suffering, Jesus was not moved from His purpose. Knowing that His death was ahead, He nevertheless trusted the strength of the Father to raise Him up. Friend, with all of this looming ahead of Jesus, if He could trust the Father, so can we. Trust empowers faith, making it immovable. Holy stands are made by trust, not by self; and we learn to take those stands and not be moved from them by trusting that the Father hears Jesus' prayers for us.

GOD'S JUDGMENT

This brings us to the second part of my chapter title, "Jesus' Fire." David dove directly into this subject after speaking of God's steadfast love. "The Lord will swallow them up in his wrath, and fire will consume them" (Psalm 21:9). This refers to all who do not enter the favor of God by receiving His free gift of salvation through Christ's finished work on the cross. If we refuse His gift, trusting in ourselves or worldly powers, our trust will fail us. The result is we'll find ourselves lost, without God's favor, hopeless, with no sanctification or protection from the enemy who comes "'to steal and kill and destroy'" (John 10:10). In short, we'll find ourselves suddenly naked and facing the fire that is Jesus.

"Your hand will find out all your enemies; your right hand will find out those who hate you" (Psalm 21:8). Twice in this verse, we read the phrase, "will find you out." If you reject Jesus, you won't be able to cover it up. The appearance of God's hand was David's way of saying, "Do you understand the crisis awaiting you? Do you grasp your impending doom? This all-consuming fire will consume you if you don't come under the favor supplied by the blood of Jesus Christ." "You will make them as a blazing oven when you appear" (Psalm 21:9).

David was foreseeing the second coming of Christ. On that day, Jesus won't come as a Baby in a manger but as a Swordsman on a white horse with tens of thousands of warrior angels. In the face of this fearsome reality, all who reject Christ's favor will feel welling up within them the force of God's wrath. The Savior bore this unbearable wrath for their sakes as well as ours, but they rejected His gift. So when the day arrives, they will have to bear that wrath themselves; and it will end with their judgment. "You will destroy their descendants from the earth, and their offspring from among the children of man" (Psalm 21:10).

Their plots and schemes will be destroyed with them. "Though they plan evil against you, though they devise mischief, they will not succeed" (Psalm 21:11). The words for "not succeed" in this verse literally mean "not be able to perform." Every vain imagining will be cast down, thwarted, and halted, brought to an end by the appearance of Jesus.

"For you will put them to flight; you will aim at their faces with your bows" (Psalm 21:12). To me, this verse pictures a fortress besieged by a marauding enemy. I envision regiments of soldiers with catapults, battering rams, and ladders used to scale high walls. I imagine this massive enemy leaping over the top to take possession of the fortress; but suddenly, they find themselves facing thousands of arrows aimed directly at them. According to verse twelve, this "will put them to flight." This is the protection Jesus gives us in His prayers. He says, in effect, "These are the things I pray for the children who will inherit my kingdom. I will put to flight every enemy that comes against them." What incredible news this is!

WHY GOD HAS TO BRING JUDGMENT AND WRATH

Verses eight through twelve of this Psalm make clear why God has to bring judgment and wrath. It is because God loves us so much. He simply wants us to escape the wrath that's going to fall upon all evil and those who commit it. This section ends by picturing God's strength destroying the enemy. His omnipotence is infinite, without measure, knowing no bounds. "Be exalted, O Lord, in your strength! We will sing and praise your power" (Psalm 21:13). This final verse of Psalm 21 returns us to the beginning, which was full of exultation over the king's strength. Those opening verses were filled with praise for the Lord's almightiness, with

David claiming, "Lord, because of You, we will not be fearful or dismayed. You are powerful on behalf of Your people!"

Jesus' prayers for us are infinitely powerful, and those prayers will accomplish His purposes. If you have turned to Him, you need not fear any weapon of the enemy, whom the Lord will turn back by His awesome strength. No Christian needs to fear falling under God's wrath because Jesus has already paid for that wrath. When He said, "'It is finished'" (John 19:30), the wrath was gone, fully absorbed in Him. Friend, you have no reason to worry about eternity. If you have trusted Jesus, He is there for you now and always.

Biography

GARY WILKERSON IS A PASTOR, author, and the president of World Challenge, an international mission organization that was founded by his father, David Wilkerson. He has traveled nationally and internationally for conferences and mission ventures, such as church plants, orphanages, clinics, and feeding programs among the poorest of the poor and most unreached people on the earth. Gary and his wife Kelly have four children and live in Colorado Springs, Colorado.

Bibliography

Spurgeon, Charles Haddon. *Spurgeon's Commentary: Hebrews.* Bellingham: Lexham Press, 2015.

Spurgeon, Charles Haddon. *The Treasury of David: Psalm Chapters 1-16.* Independently Published, 2017.

Also Available From Gary Wilkerson and Ambassador International

Most of us know Who Jesus is and would admit that He was a good and kind Teacher while here on earth. But He is so much more—He is our Savior and God and worthy of all our worship. Through an in-depth study into the book of Hebrews, Joshua West and Gary Wilkerson take apart each verse, drawing the reader to a closer look at the Man Who lived here on earth for a short time. If you are searching for something more from God, dive into this study and drink in the jaw-dropping beauty of our Jesus.

How do you pray to God with complete honesty about your struggles? When the Lord's plans for your life seem completely derailed, how do you approach the Father with your heartache and anger? There are so few guidelines for these types of prayers in the modern church, but the Bible offers us an entire book of examples to follow and a road to follow toward healing.

In the first volume of this devotional series, Gary Wilkerson, pastor and president of World Challenge, examines the first twelve psalms and how each is a unique invitation to authentic prayer. Our heavenly Father desires a deep, genuine relationship with each one of us, but that can happen only if we are completely transparent with God about our doubts, struggles, and sorrows."

This book is published in association with World Challenge.

Transforming lives through the message and mission of Jesus Christ.

For more information about
WORLD CHALLENGE
and
The Generation That Seeks the Lord
please visit:

www.worldchallenge.org

Ambassador International's mission is to magnify the Lord Jesus Christ and promote His Gospel through the written word.

We believe through the publication of Christian literature, Jesus Christ and His Word will be exalted, believers will be strengthened in their walk with Him, and the lost will be directed to Jesus Christ as the only way of salvation.

For more information about
AMBASSADOR INTERNATIONAL
please visit:

www.ambassador-international.com
@AmbassadorIntl
www.facebook.com/AmbassadorIntl

AMBASSADOR INTERNATIONAL
GREENVILLE, SOUTH CAROLINA & BELFAST, NORTHERN IRELAND

www.ambassador-international.com
Magnifying Jesus while promoting His gospel through the written word.

www.ingramcontent.com/pod-product-compliance
Lightning Source LLC
Chambersburg PA
CBHW062102080426
42734CB00012B/2721